P9-ECJ-513

Graphis Inc. is committed to presenting exceptional work in international Design, Advertising, Illustration & Photography.

Graphis Advertising Annual 2014

Published by **Graphis** | Publisher & Creative Director: **B. Martin Pedersen** | Executive Assistant: **Sara Allen** | Designer: **Hee Ra Kim**

Editor: **Rachel Lowry** | Production: **Tiffany Washington** | Web & Project Manager: **Mark Watkins** | Web Developer: **Scott Meisburger**

Remarks: We extend our heartfelt thanks to contributors throughout the world who have made it possible to publish a wide and international spectrum of the best work in this field. Entry instructions for all Graphis Books may be requested from: Graphis Inc., 114 West 17th Street, Second Floor, New York, New York 10011, or visit our web site at www.graphis.com.

Anmerkungen: Unser Dank gilt den Einsendern aus aller Welt, die es uns ermöglicht haben, ein breites, internationales. Spekt-rum der besten Arbeiten zu veröffentlichen. Teilnahmebedingungen für die GraphisBücher sind erhältlich bei: Graphis, Inc., 114 West 17th Street, Second Floor, New York, New York 10011. Besuchen Sie uns im World Wide Web, www.graphis.com.

Remerciements: Nous remercions les participants du monde entier qui ont rendu possible la publication de cet ouvrage offrant un panorama complet des meilleurs travaux. Les modalités d'inscription peuvent être obtenues auprès de: Graphis, Inc., 114 West 17th Street, Second Floor, New York, New York 10011. Rendez-nous visite sur notre site web: www.graphis.com.

© Copyright under universal copyright convention copyright © 2013 by Graphis, Inc., 114 West 17th Street, Second Floor, New York, New York 10011. Jacket and book design copyright © 2013 by Graphis, Inc. No part of this book may be reproduced, utilized or transmitted in any form without written permission of the publisher. ISBN: 978-1-932026-86-3. Printed in Croatia.

Contents

The Americas

Arnold Eidus
*Advertising Executive
and Concert Violinist*
1922-2013

Bob Levenson
Advertising Executive
1929-2013

Bryce Courtenay
Advertising Executive
1933-2012

David Deutsch
Advertising Executive
1957-2013

David N. Martin
Ad Agency Founder
1930-2012

Don Keller
Creative Director
1928-2013

Erwin Harris
Advertising Executive
1921-2013

George Friedman
Advertising Executive
1935-2012

Glenn Mason
Advertising Executive
1915-2013

Glenn Tintera
Advertising Executive
1931-2013

Jennifer Rosoff
Advertising Executive
1978-2013

John Olson
Ad Agency Founder
1956-2013

Maxwell Arnold
Advertising Executive
1919-2013

Michael J. Roarty
Advertising Executive
1928-2013

Mike Roarty
Advertising Executive
1928-2013

Patrick McGrath
Advertising Executive
1934-2013

Peter Carter
Advertising Executive
1943-2013

Robert H. Levenson
Advertising Executive
1929-2013

Shirley Riley-Davis
Advertising Executive
1935-2013

Stephen Frankfurt
Advertising Executive
1931-12012

Asia

Li Yuan
Advertising Executive
1988-2013

Yoshiharu Fujii
Advertising Executive
1959-2013

Europe

Andy Carolan
Advertising Executive
1961-2012

Chris Cowpe
Advertising Executive
1951-2013

Rhys Davies
Advertising Executive
1990-2012

Opposite page: *White Triumphator Tulip, from joSon: Intimate Portraits of Nature*

The grandson of a prolific impressionist painter, John Payne has always liked to build and create. Sometimes it's vintage bikes or muscle cars in his garage, which he says is more of a studio. But most of the time, it's brands. Payne launched his career at The Richards Group in Texas, which ultimately led to a position with Saatchi & Saatchi, LA, where he is currently Creative Director. There, he has worked on numerous major brands ranging from Levi's to Whiskas, winning awards with the Cannes Film Festival, D&AD and the One Show. His specialty? Anything with wheels.

When and what first influenced you to become an art director?

My grandfather was a painter. That had a big influence on me He was pretty prolific, and his work is still circulating. But he never saw any financial success while he was alive. I think that's partly why I never really had any interest in being a traditional artist. I didn't want to be a "starving" artist. I always knew I wanted to be in a job that involved creativity. Advertising is what I found, and I love it. It sounds silly, but another thing that influenced my decision to become an art director was that old television show "Bewitched." I grew up watching it, and I thought Darren Stevens had a really cool job. He was an art director at the agency, McMann & Tate.

Who would be an ideal employee for you?

There are two types of candidates I prefer. I like kids coming right out of school, and I like people who have proven themselves and know what they're doing. Kids coming out of school are full of energy, enthusiasm and creativity. They're not jaded yet. And they usually have a pretty good attitude and work ethic because they're trying to prove themselves. The senior people are great because they can just hit the ground running. They don't require too much supervision. They just get it done. It's the people in the middle that are a pain in the ass. They think they have it all figured out, but they usually don't. They're also the most likely to be lazy and apathetic, two traits I cannot tolerate. But I like anybody with enthusiasm and a creative mind. It doesn't really matter what level they are.

What part of your job do you find most demanding?

It's all about the ideas. Coming up with them. Developing them. And protecting them. Those are the big challenges. But if the idea is sound, rooted in strategy and presented in a unique way, developing it and protecting it is a lot easier. If an idea doesn't campaign out easily, then it's probably a one-off idea. If it's constantly under attack and needs too much protection, it's probably off strategy. Clients are much braver when work is on strategy. So I guess the most demanding part of my job is coming up with the ideas. Everything else is about support.

How do you set up an agency environment that fosters creativity?

I started my career at the Richards Group in Dallas, TX. It was a very structured agency with strict rules on everything from punctuality to how we dressed. I spent five years there. In spite of all the rules, it was a great place to work. And we were doing great work.

My next job was at Chiat/Day in Los Angeles. Chiat was the complete opposite. It was chaotic. There was structure, but it was loose. And you didn't know the rules until you broke them. Both places fostered creativity, and each had their pros and cons. I think the one thing they had in common was a sick work ethic and a strong drive to create fresh work that was beautifully crafted.

The secret to fostering creativity is to let people do their thing. No one likes to be over managed. You give people freedom to explore. Let them make mistakes and fall down every once in a while and great things happen. When you have that kind of mentality, it frees people up to be more creative. If they're always worried about failing, they won't take chances and the work will be safe, expected and boring.

Is it possible to manage creative people and also create your own work?

Yes, but it's a tricky balance. As a creative director, I try to be more of an enabler and an influencer than a competitor. Sometimes I have more influence than others. It depends on the project. If a team is on target and getting it done, I stay out of the way and try to clear the path for

them. If a team is struggling, I step in and help them make the work better. Occasionally, I'll give them an idea and let them run with it. But I never compete against them.

Who was your past mentor in advertising?
I spent ten years at Chiat/Day and was lucky enough to work with Lee Clow on several projects. Lee is an incredibly smart guy. But he doesn't let it get in the way. He keeps it simple, always. He's got amazing focus and clarity. He takes in all the information and distills it down to a simple premise. That allows him to look at a wall covered in ideas and pick the one that will become a famous campaign. I've seen him do it over and over again. He's got a knack for spotting great work, work that creates a movement. And I think his secret is simple. He doesn't let all the bullshit cloud his judgment. He only concentrates on the stuff that really matters and leaves the rest behind. I'll spend the rest of my career trying to master that.
The other guy I must mention is Rob Lawton. He was one of my instructors in portfolio school. Rob is a designer. But, above all, he is a conceptual thinker. The guy is legendary. He's one of the most talented and passionate people I've ever met. When he liked something, it was a huge deal. He was very picky. I'm still practicing his lessons today. And if he was still teaching, I'd sign up for another class.

Who do you admire most in the advertising profession?
It may sound cliché, but if I gotta pick one person, it's Bill Bernbach. He revolutionized our business. Before him, advertising was stiff and boring. Bernbach changed everything. He turned advertising into an art form. I probably wouldn't be in this business if Bill Bernbach hadn't done what he did back in the 1960s.

Aside from advertising, what do you do with your free time?
I spend a lot of time in the garage. It's my refuge. I can be creative there. And I don't have to worry about deadlines or what anybody else thinks. I've got a couple old motorcycles, an old car and a few old bicycles that I'm usually working on. It's set up more like a studio than a garage. It's a pretty great place to hang out.

What is your creative approach and/or philosophy?
It's pretty simple. I look for the truth in things, something that connects with people. What makes it relevant? What makes it different, unique? Then I look for an interesting way to present that point. Sometimes it can be done with an interesting visual solution, sometimes with a well-written line. But there's always a concept. It doesn't really matter what the project is. People appreciate conceptual solutions. They may not know it, but they do. There are so many things competing for their attention these days. If you don't have something interesting to say, and you don't present it in an interesting way, you don't stand a chance.

How much should you rely on intuition and gut feeling?
If you don't have intuition and gut instincts in advertising, you're in the wrong business. It takes experience and knowledge to know what to listen to and what to ignore. But if you've done your homework; understanding the consumer, the product you're pushing and the business objective, then intuition is a powerful force. It's usually right.

What is your prediction for the future of advertising?
That's a tough question. I don't think advertising is going anywhere. It's been around since the stone age. Early man used his cave wall to advertise the animals he hunted. Today, we advertise prepackaged hamburgers on computer screens and mobile devices. As long as we have civilization and commerce, we'll have advertising. The media is constantly changing, and we gotta keep up with it. But ideas/concepts aren't going anywhere. When that's gone, so am I.

What is your personal philosophy on good advertising?
Good advertising is good communication. It finds a creative way to reach people. Sometimes it's done with stunning visuals, and sometimes it's done with 140 characters. The medium doesn't really matter. It's all about what you're saying and how you're saying it. If it's delivering a relevant message in a meaningful way, I consider it good advertising. If it does it in a way that touches people in a profound way and starts a movement, then it's great advertising.

If the advertising is good and touches people in a profound way, and starts a movement, then it's great advertising.

John Payne *Creative Director, Saatchi & Saatchi, LA*

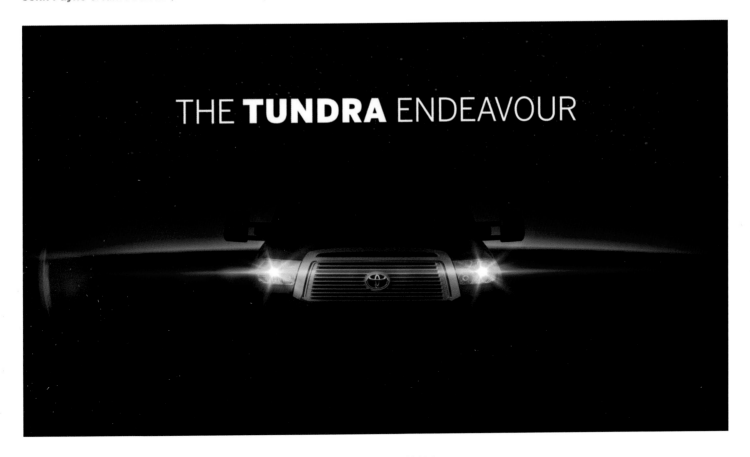

For Jera Mehrdad, a pen has always fit comfortably in hand. Though she has been drawing and designing things since she can remember, the decision to go into graphic design — and later advertising — was influenced by a high school graphic design class. Jera launched her career as Art Director for Cramer-Krasselt, TBWA\Chiat\Day and later Innocean Worldwide, before becoming Associate Creative Director for Saatchi & Saatchi. She has worked on a variety of brands, including Pedigree, Energizer, ASICS, Hyundai and now Toyota. When she's not whittling away on the computer, Mehrdad enjoys having dance parties in her living room with her husband, two daughters and two big dogs.

What was the biggest risk you have taken? What was the result and was it worth it?
Probably the biggest risk I have taken was moving from Phoenix to Los Angeles to take a job at TBWA\Chiat\Day after I just had a baby. I went from working at a pretty laid back place to one of the best and most hectic agencies. I was scared that I wouldn't be able to juggle the intensity of being at a great agency and being a mom, but it proved to be a great experience and a really creative time for me. I was around some of the best creatives in the business working on some fun campaigns. So, it was definitely worth it.

What is your definition of good advertising?
I love advertising that makes you feel something. Whether you are laughing out loud or being inspired to think about things in a new way, the best advertising gives a brand an emotional meaning.

What inspires you?
Almost anything inspires me. I'm sometimes inspired by really silly things. Like, I find inspiration in how cartoonish flamingos look in real life. Then there's the obvious inspiration like beautiful art, my daughters and amazing stories.

What are your favorite typefaces?
I really love typography in general. I think almost all typefaces can be beautiful, but I'd say my favorite are more modern looking san serif faces. I really love Helvetica Neue.

How did this project evolve from a concept to a finished product?
The new Avalon was a big deal to Toyota so there was a lot of expectations to do something great and breakthrough. We had played in a lot of different spaces, but in the end we wanted to make it all about the car. And we wanted to find a new way to do it. We took inspiration in the designers who created it. One of them had mentioned that the car wasn't mechanical, it was sculpted by artists. We were inspired by that, so we researched different kinds of artistic techniques that could create a car in a beautiful way. We created TV, Print and interactive ads that showed the Avalon being created from art. We wanted it to be memorable and iconic. Hopefully, it achieved that.

Copy-driven vs. image-based advertising? Which do you prefer?
As long as it's good, either way can work. I'll refer back to my definition of good advertising. If it makes you feel something, it's good. I'm a sucker for anything that looks good. So, if a long copy ad is well art directed and well-written, I'll love it. If the ad has amazing imagery that corollates to the concept, I'll love it too. Yes, it's kind of a cop out, but really, good is good.

When you start a project, what is your plan that helps insure success?
These days, it's collaboration. Although we are always thinking more creatively, there's a logic and business to creating ads. The more that you solidify your ideas to strategic insights, work with media to buy the right placements and understand the right things to bring to the client, the more success you'll have at selling good work. If all links in the chain feel they're a part of the idea, they are more willing to fight to sell it. That sounds pretty business-y, but that has really helped me.

Do you consider advertising to be an art, a science or both?
There is definitely an art and a science to advertising. A lot of it is really problem-solving, but when you do it in a really creative way, it's art.

What will spark the next "Creative Revolution" in advertising?
I think content is ever evolving, so it's hard to say. It always boils down to a good idea. No matter whatever is 'next,' a good idea and a strong message will always be revolutionary.

What advice would you give to a student entering the profession today?
My advice to future creatives would be to work hard. Never be too good for an assignment. Be humble and be hungry.

There is definitely an art and a science to advertising. A lot of it is really problem solving, but when you do it in a really creative way, it's art.

Jera Mehrdad *Associate Creative Director, Saatchi & Saatchi, LA*

Matthew Poitras got his start in advertising through a casual encounter with the Executive Creative Director of Modernista at a bar in Boston. Seriously. The now-Associate Creative Director at Saatchi & Saatchi, LA says they taught him everything he knows. He would later become one of the head writers for Cadillac and a designer for Leo Burnett and Amalgamated NYC. Poitras makes weird sculptures and says his spirit animal is the salamander.

What award shows do you have respect for in the industry?

The Effies. Back when I worked at Arnold we had the TED people come to lecture us on how to make good advertising. They basically showed us a bunch of hipster stuff for the 18-35 male crowd and said "do that". Ironically, a lot of the people in the audience actually worked on that stuff. I'm normally the artsy guy, but I stood up and asked the woman how effective those campaigns were. She was annoyed. Right then I dropped all platitudes about why we're here. We sell products, hopefully in a beautiful way that helps people. Goofy surrealism be damned.

How do you set up an agency environment that fosters creativity?

It always comes from the ECD. You need a leader who joins the fight, creatively. Someone you respect as an artist. Someone with a vision. That makes things a lot easier.

Is it possible to both manage creative people and create your own work?

Yes. The key is to realize this is a lifestyle job and we spend a lot of time together. When you realize you sort of live or die by each others' work it makes it easier to shut off the ego and just flow. I think that's where the best work comes from. Selfless sharing and caring

Who was your past mentor in advertising?

Lance Jenson from Arnold. He did a lot of that great VW work. "Pink Moon" etc… His secret? Make music a priority and convince your client not to do testing.

What is your creative approach\philosophy?

Start by exploring what you absolutely shouldn't do. Start blowing out your most counter-intuitive thoughts. I usually find they're pretty juicy ideas.

Do you consider advertising to be art, science or both?

There's a Warhol interview where he says an artist is just any-body who's really good at what they do. The interviewer said "Oh yeah, well what's art then?". He goes, "Whatever you can get away with." So yeah, I guess it's art.

What will spark the next creative revolution in advertising?

A bad economy taking down some of the big clients. This will make new "challenger" brands who's edge will be their storytelling. It's already happening.

What would you say to creatives entering the industry today?

Align yourself with brands and businesses that put a stake in the ground. Never try to please everybody or you'll go schizophrenic.

Do you think advertising creators have a responsibility to the public?

Absolutely. Everybody does, especially those of us with access to the airwaves. Not to sound shrewd, but altruism helps the bottom line. The high road works in many ways.

Align yourself with brands and businesses that put a stake in the ground. Never try to please everybody or you'll go schizophrenic.

Matthew Poitras *Associate Creative Director, Saatchi & Saatchi, LA*

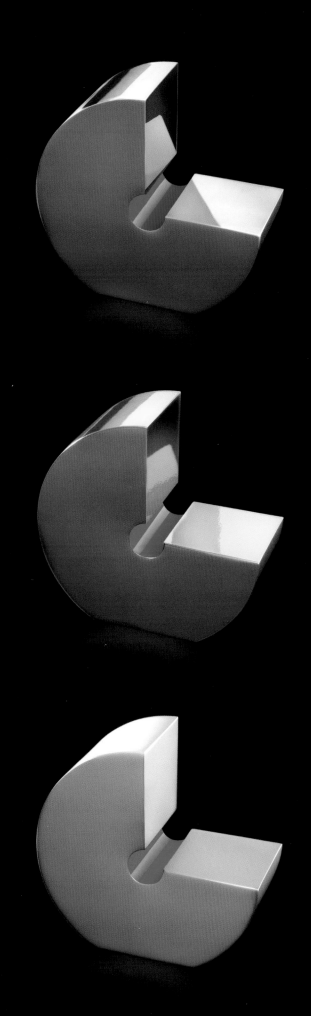

YOU CAN'T STOP AN IDEA
WHOSE TIME HAS COME.

THE RADICALLY NEW AVALON
A game changer in the art of making cars, and an exciting
new landmark for the future of driving as we know it.

Agency: **Saatchi & Saatchi, LA** | Client: **Toyota Avalon** | Page: **16**

Agency: **LLOYD&CO** | Client: **Adidas** | Page: **70**

Agency: **Publicis Kaplan Thaler**
Client: **P&G/ Crest 3D White Strips** | Page: **44**

Agency: **Butler, Shine, Stern & Partners** | Client: **MINI Global** | Page: **216**

Agency: **PP+K** | Client: **Big Cat Rescue**
Page: **155**

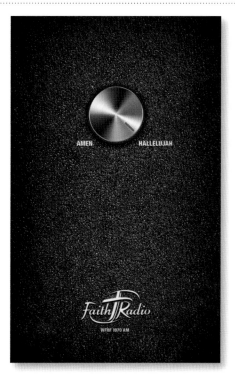

Agency: **BRIGHT RED\TBWA**
Client: **Faith Radio** | Page: **51**

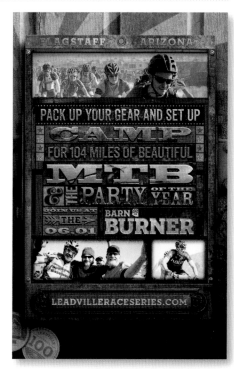

Agency: **3e The Life Time Agency**
Client: **Life Time - The Healthy Way of Life Company** | Page: **65**

THE RADICALLY NEW AVALON
A game changer in the art of making cars, and an exciting
new landmark for the future of driving as we know it.

TOYOTA | Let's Go Places

YOU CAN'T STOP AN IDEA
WHOSE TIME HAS COME.

Saatchi & Saatchi, LA | Toyota Avalon

YOU CAN'T STOP AN IDEA
WHOSE TIME HAS COME.

THE RADICALLY NEW **AVALON**

A game changer in the art of making cars, and an exciting
new landmark for the future of driving as we know it.

Saatchi & Saatchi, LA | Toyota Avalon

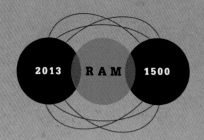

25 MPG HIGHWAY

0%

BODY FAT

5-YEAR/100,000-MILE POWERTRAIN WARRANTY

BEST-IN-CLASS HWY FUEL ECONOMY THE PIONEERING COMBINATION OF THE 3.6L PENTASTAR® V6 WITH AN EIGHT-SPEED TRANSMISSION OFFERS 6,500 POUNDS OF TOWING POWER, 160 MORE MILES PER TANK, AND THE BEST HIGHWAY FUEL ECONOMY OF ANY TRUCK IN ITS CLASS. THE NEW 2013 RAM 1500. ENGINEERED TO MOVE HEAVEN AND EARTH.

Standard pickup class, excludes hybrid models. EPA est. 17 city/20 comb/25 hwy mpg based on V6 4x2. V8 with EPA est. 14 city/20 hwy mpg shown. See dealer for copy of the powertrain limited warranty. Ram is a trademark of Chrysler Group LLC.

f RAMTRUCKS.COM

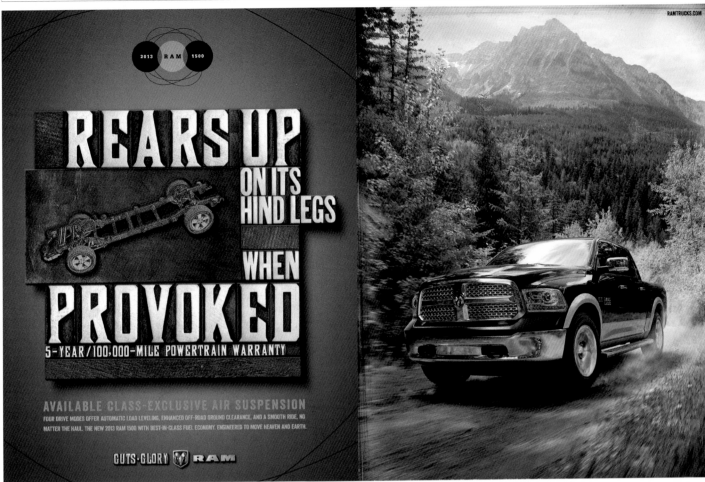

PERMIT TO SHIP GAME FISH

COME BACK WITH BIGGER STORIES

2013

PERMIT TO SHIP GAME FISH

ASK AGENT FOR FREE DIGEST OF FISHING LAWS

2013
RAM 1500 OUTDOORSMAN

B G 4727

RESIDENT FISHING LICENSE

STANDARD CLASS IV TRAILER HITCH & TRAILER WIRING HOOKUP	
NEW PENTASTAR® V6 & TORQUEFLITE™ 8-SPEED AUTOMATIC	
AVAILABLE ACTIVE-LEVEL™ 4-CORNER AIR SUSPENSION	
BEST-IN-CLASS 4X4 FUEL ECONOMY	ON/OFF-ROAD TIRES
5-YEAR/100,000-MILE POWERTRAIN WARRANTY	4 ✓ 7 ✓

GUTS·GLORY RAM

RAMTRUCKS.COM

STANDARD PICKUP CLASS, EXCLUDES HYBRIDS. EPA ESTIMATED 16 CITY/19 COMB/23 HWY 4X4 V6. PENTASTAR V6 OUTDOORSMAN LATE AVAILABILITY. SEE YOUR DEALER FOR A COPY OF THE POWERTRAIN LIMITED WARRANTY. RAM IS A REGISTERED TRADEMARK OF CHRYSLER GROUP LLC.

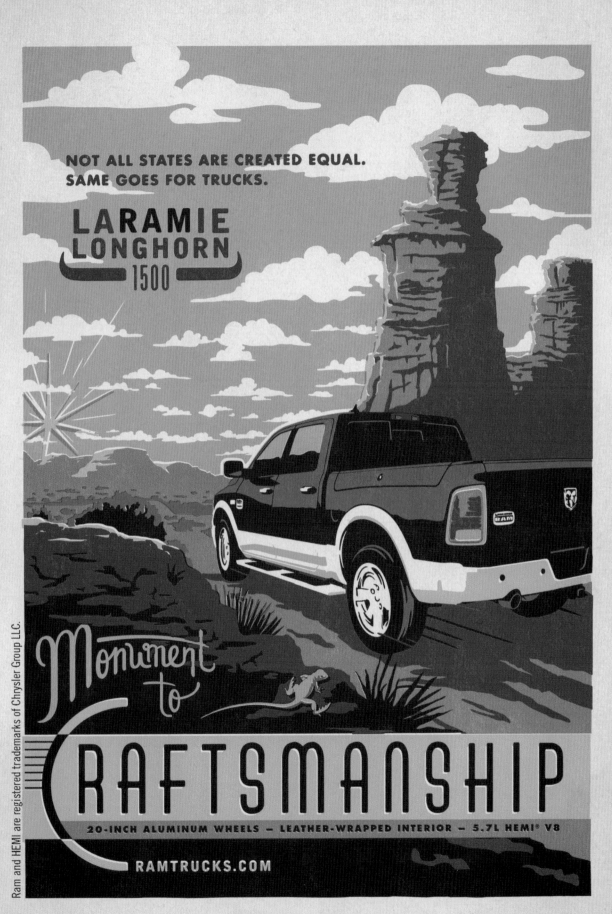

The Richards Group | Ram

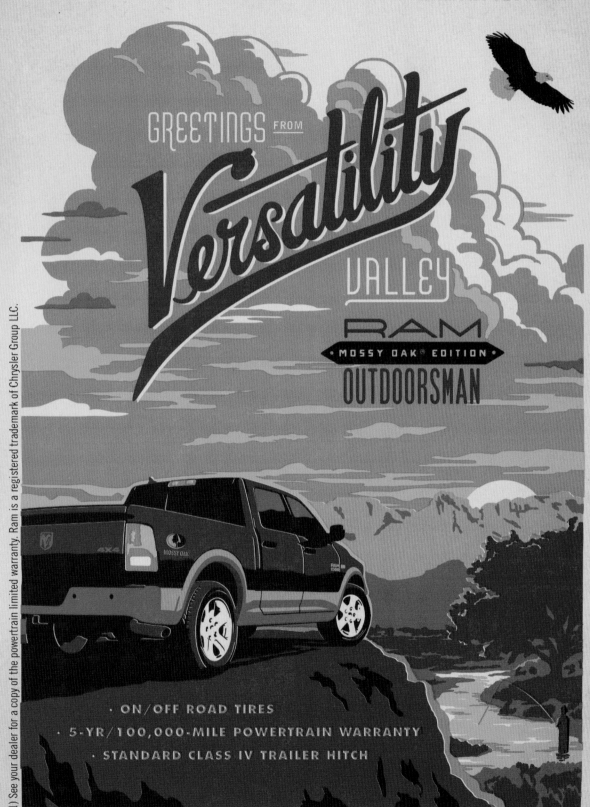

IRRESISTIBLE.

THE NEW BMW Z4.

IRRESISTIBLE.

THE NEW BMW Z4.

BMW Z4

www.bmw.co.th

**The Ultimate
Driving Machine**

Lewis Communications | Tiffin Motorhomes

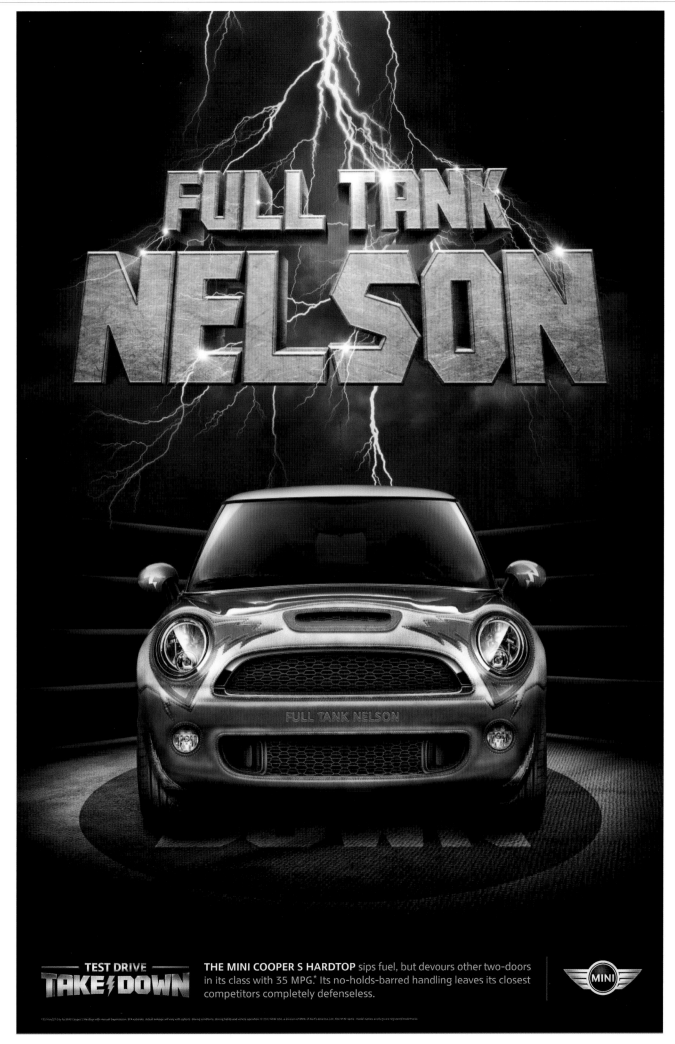

Butler, Shine, Stern & Partners | MINI USA

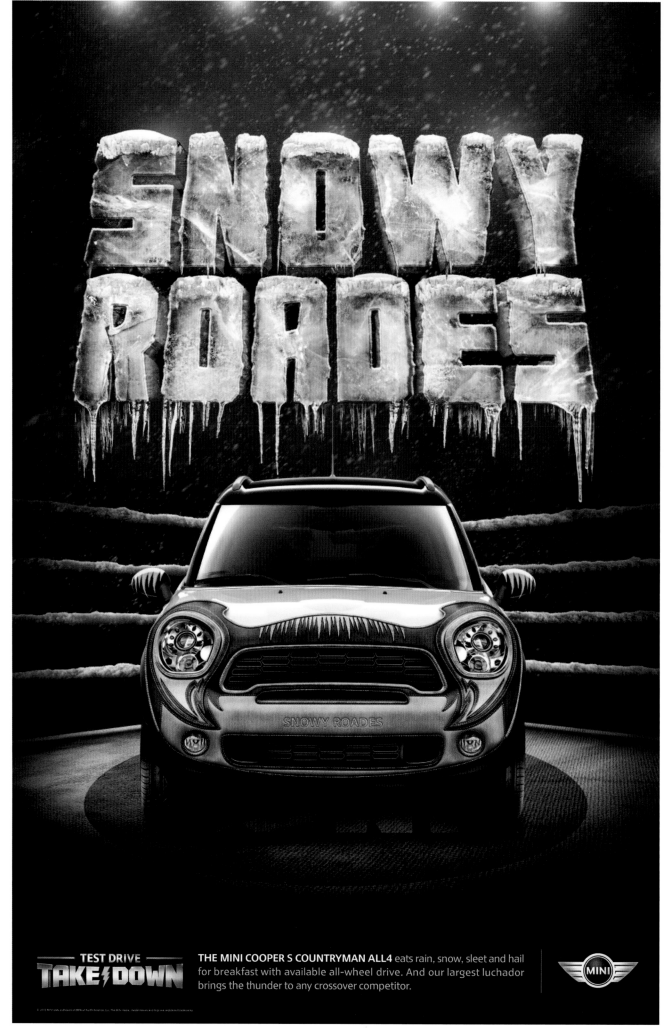

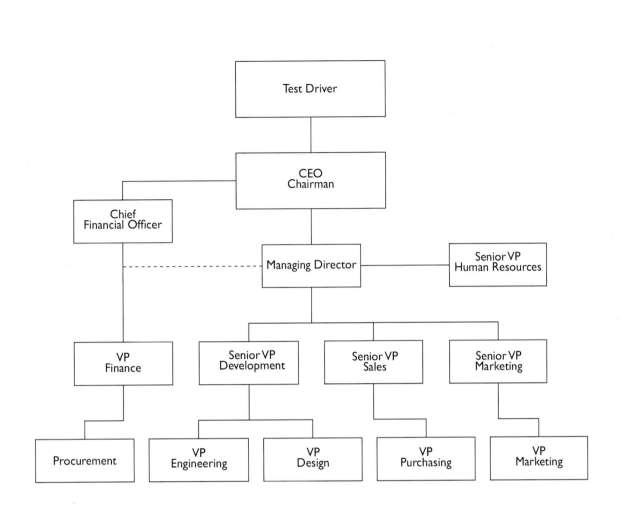

```
                    ┌──────────────┐
                    │ Test Driver  │
                    └──────┬───────┘
                           │
                    ┌──────┴───────┐
                    │     CEO      │
                    │   Chairman   │
                    └──────┬───────┘
          ┌────────────────┤
  ┌───────┴────────┐       │
  │     Chief      │       │
  │Financial Officer│      │
  └───────┬────────┘       │
          │         ┌───────────────┐        ┌──────────────────┐
          ┆---------│Managing Director│──────│    Senior VP     │
          │         └───────┬───────┘        │ Human Resources  │
          │                 │                └──────────────────┘
  ┌───────┴──┐  ┌───────────┼──────────┬────────────┐
  │    VP    │  │ Senior VP │ Senior VP│  Senior VP  │
  │ Finance  │  │Development│   Sales  │  Marketing  │
  └───────┬──┘  └─────┬─────┴──────────┴─────────────┘
          │           │
```

| Procurement | VP Engineering | VP Design | VP Purchasing | VP Marketing |

At Saab, performance is always Number One.

SAAB

PP+K | Tires Plus

TIRES INSTALLED IN UNDER AN HOUR. **GUARANTEED.**

We'll install your tires in 59 minutes or less with an appointment, or you get $59 back and a free oil change.

Our Ecopia Tires are so eco-friendly and fuel efficient that even nature prefers them.

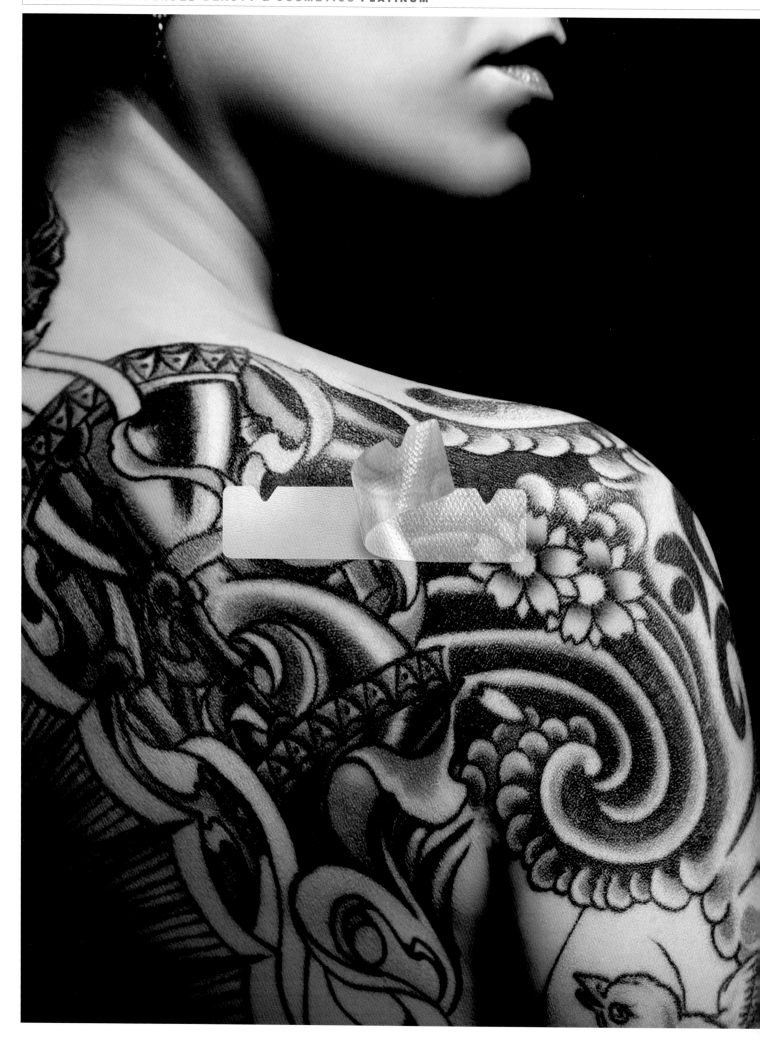

As nature intended

As nature intended

Publicis Kaplan Thaler | P&G/ Crest 3D White Strips

omdr Co.,Ltd. | MTG Co.,Ltd.

Glamure

目元にみなぎるハリ、高純質プラセンタの自信。

MTG
We have many dreams

AMEN HALLELUJAH

WFRF 1070 AM

BRIGHT RED\TBWA | Faith Radio

Six ways Dodge builds your business

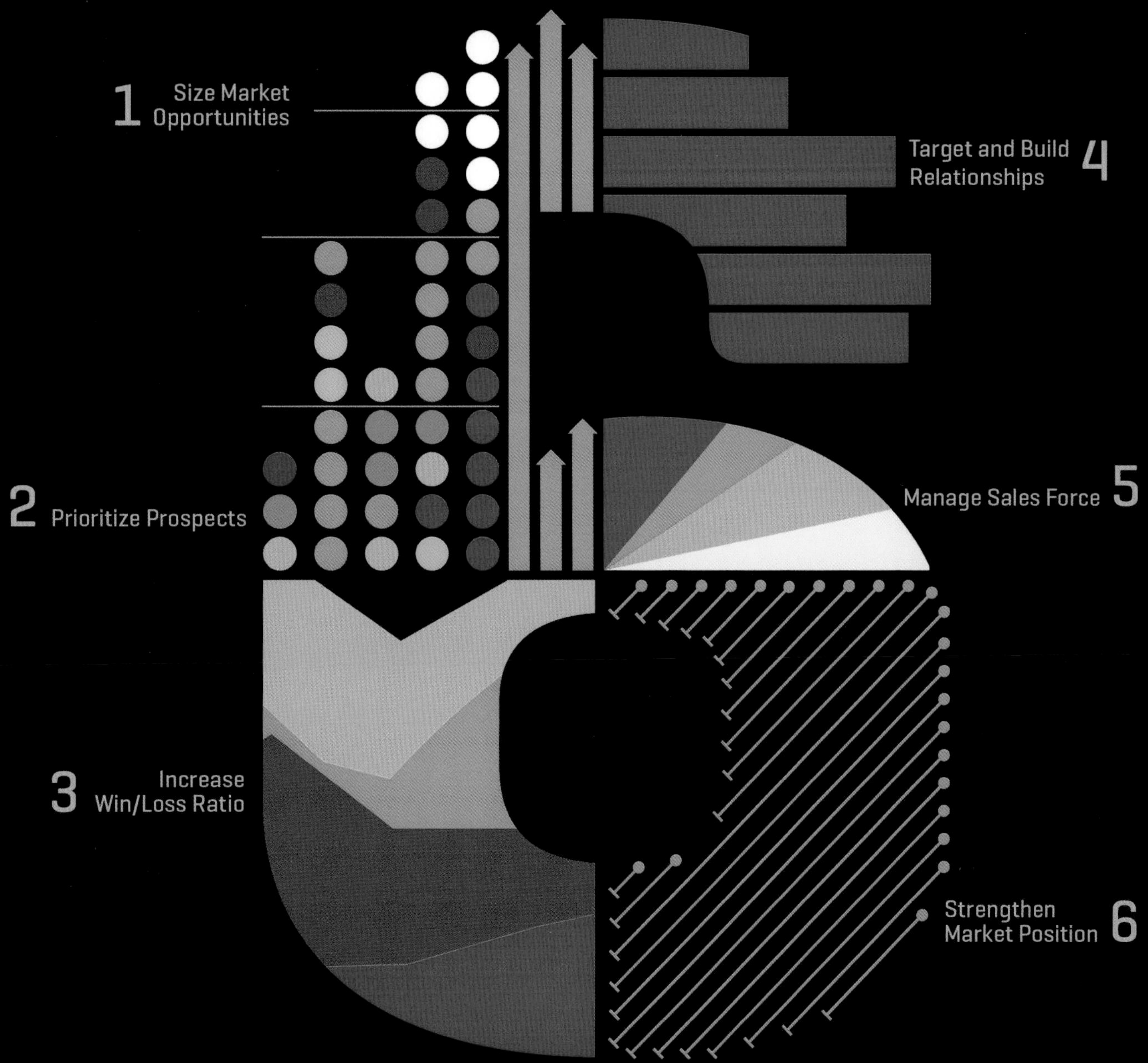

1 Size Market Opportunities

2 Prioritize Prospects

3 Increase Win/Loss Ratio

Target and Build Relationships 4

Manage Sales Force 5

Strengthen Market Position 6

DODGE

Essential intelligence to build on

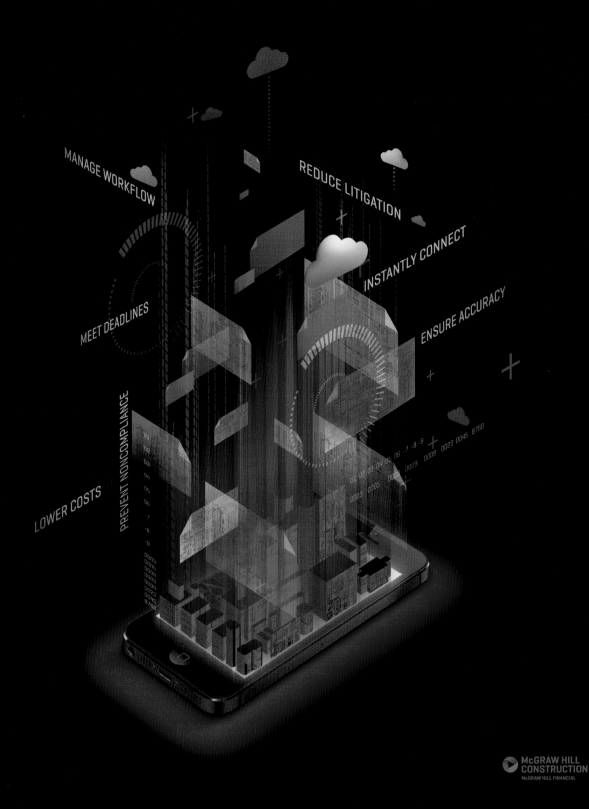

Introducing

DODGE DocuPro™

Control the Documents. Control the Project.

Chaos loves construction. But now, chaos will be locked out of your jobs. Because now, you have Dodge DocuPro. Integrated with the Dodge Network, it gives you total document control, from design through completion.

For a free consultation and ROI analysis, call 855-237-4413 or visit DodgeDocuPro.com

MANAGE WORKFLOW

REDUCE LITIGATION

INSTANTLY CONNECT

MEET DEADLINES

ENSURE ACCURACY

PREVENT NONCOMPLIANCE

LOWER COSTS

McGRAW HILL CONSTRUCTION
McGRAW HILL FINANCIAL

being accepted: **priceless**

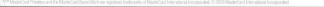

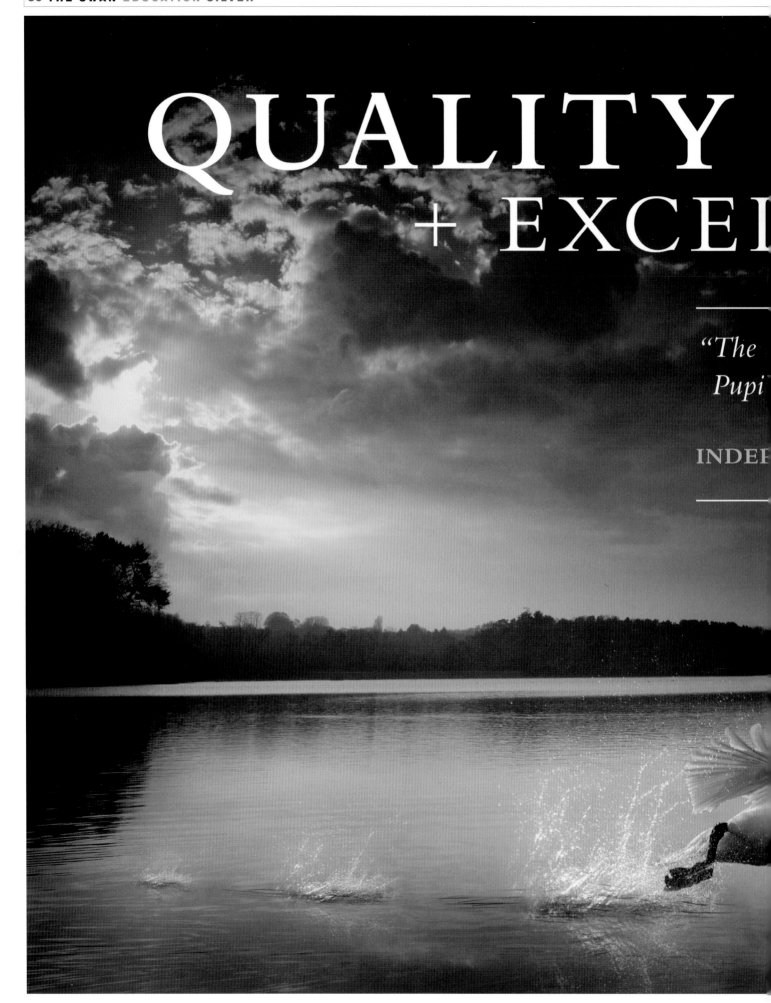

QUALITY
+ EXCEL

"The
Pupi

INDEF

LENCE

...ality of academic and other achievements is excellent.
...are very well educated...they aim high and achieve well."

NDENT SCHOOLS INSPECTORATE – OCTOBER 2012

KING'S BRUTON

Deo Juvante

Ice House Design | Ian & Helen Wilmshurst. King's School, Bruton

FALL, 1849

Judge R. E. B. Baylor and another trustee of Baylor University, Judge Abner S. Lipscomb of the Supreme Court of the State of Texas, begin teaching classes in the "science of law." In 1857, Baylor will open the first law school in Texas. Judge Baylor will teach Constitutional Law there until his death in 1873.

For over 170 years, great institutions have shared more than a vision, they've shared a name. They still do.

BAYLOR

SPRING, 1929

Justin Ford Kimball, Executive VP of Baylor University Hospital in Dallas, notices that Dallas teachers owe many of the hospital's bad debts. Kimball creates the Baylor Plan, a way for them to pay just 50 cents a month for health insurance. Teachers eagerly join, paving the way for the Blue Cross prepayment plan. By 1933, voluntary health insurance is embraced by the American Hospital Association as a solution for financing health care for Americans.

For over 170 years, great institutions have shared more than a vision, they've shared a name. They still do.

BAYLOR

APRIL 21, 1966

Michael Ellis DeBakey, world-renowned cardiac surgeon, innovator, professor and Chairman of the Department of Surgery at the Baylor College of Medicine, is the first in the world to use an external left heart pump successfully in a patient. He will later pioneer development of the artificial heart and help invent over 70 surgical instruments, changing the course of medicine forever.

For over 170 years, great institutions have shared more than a vision, they've shared a name. They still do.

BAYLOR

FEBRUARY 1, 1841

Judge R. E. B. Baylor, William Tryon and James Huckins gather in a small, simple building near Rutersville to discuss establishing an institution that "...would be fully susceptible of enlargement and development to meet the needs of all the ages to come." Amidst frontier raids, yellow fever epidemics and bandits, that institution will be chartered in 1845, making it the first institution of higher learning in Texas. An institution known today as Baylor University.

For over 170 years, great institutions have shared more than a vision, they've shared a name. They still do.

BAYLOR

FEBRUARY 24, 1944

First Lieutenant Mary Louise Roberts, a Baylor nurse
in charge of a surgical tent at the 56th Evacuation
Hospital Unit on the beach of Anzio, Italy, comes under
fire from German artillery. Nicknamed "Hell's Half Acre"
because of the relentless shelling and murderous
shrapnel, the tent begins to catch fire. In total darkness,
Lt. Roberts and her staff evacuate 42 patients from
the blazing tent by flashlight. For this, she will become
the first woman to earn the Silver Star.

For over 170 years,
great institutions have shared more than a vision,
they've shared a name. They still do.

BAYLOR

SCHOOLYARD.

Introducing the Architectural Record CEU App. The only app that allows you to fulfill credits and track your progress without Internet access.

Download free at iTunes.

LIBRARY.

Introducing the Architectural Record CEU App. The only app that allows you to fulfill credits and track your progress without Internet access.

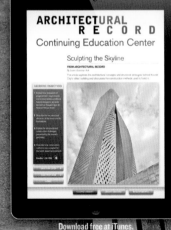

Download free at iTunes.

LECTURE HALL.

Introducing the Architectural Record CEU App. The only app that allows you to fulfill credits and track your progress without Internet access.

ARCHITECTURAL RECORD
Continuing Education Center

Sculpting the Skyline

FROM ARCHITECTURAL RECORD
By Joann Gonchar, AIA

The article explores the architectural concepts and structural strategies behind Kuwait City's tallest building and discusses the construction methods used to build it.

LEARNING OBJECTIVES

1 Explain how evolution of programmatic requirements and environmental conditions helped designers generate the form of Kuwait City's Al Hamra Firdous Tower.

2 Describe the key structural elements of the tower and its foundations.

3 Explain the structural and construction challenges presented by the tower's geometry.

4 Describe how construction methods were adapted for the harsh desert environment.

Credits: 1.00 HSW

SAVE FOR LATER

TAKE TEST NOW

HOME

COURSE LIBRARY | CREDIT TRACKER | REQUIREMENTS

Download free at iTunes.

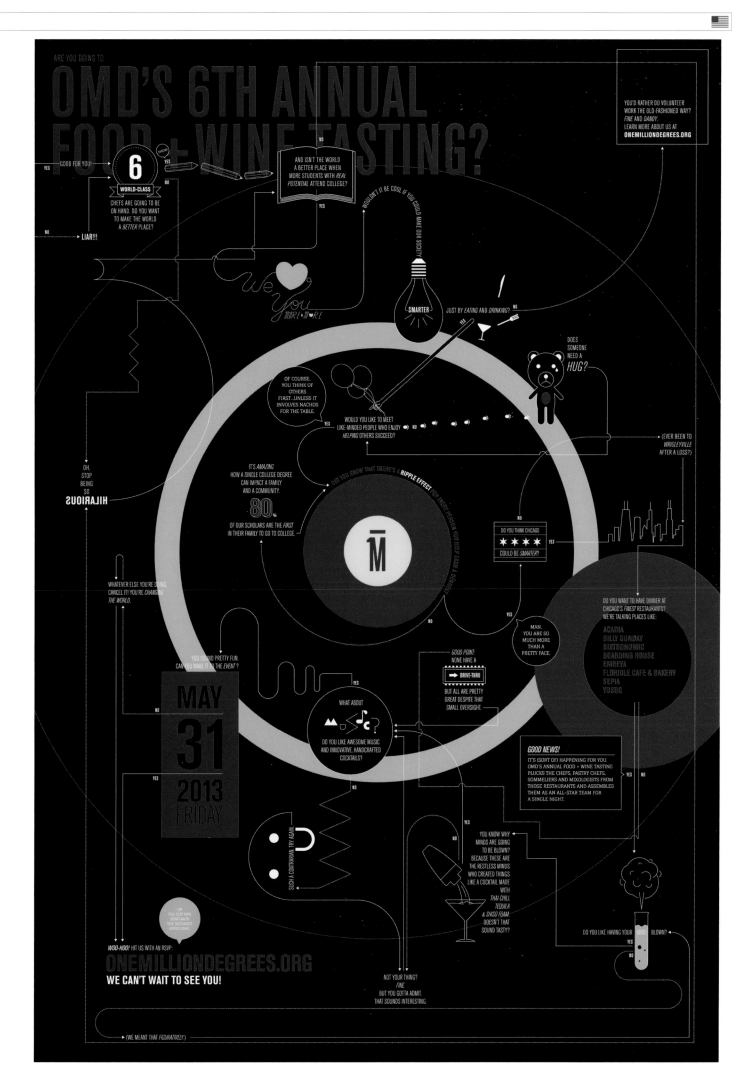

ADVENTURE ISN'T A *REHEARSAL*. PREPARE *ACCORDINGLY*.

FindMeSPOT.com

YOUR MOMENT OF A LIFETIME IS WAITING.

Challenge a hill. Conquer a trail. Or get as far off the beaten path as you want. The new SPOT Gen3 and SPOT Global Phone will keep you connected with family, friends and emergency assistance when you're outside cellular coverage. Even share your location via GPS in real time. Start your adventure at **FindMeSPOT.com.**

Ready for Adventure

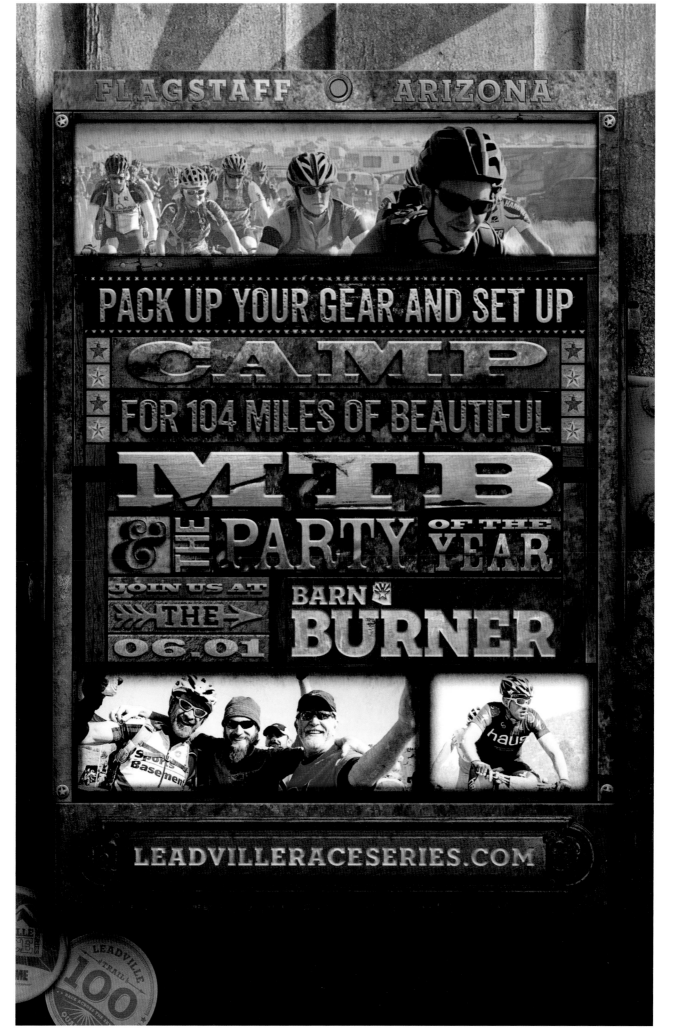

Wong, Doody, Crandall, Wiener | Seattle International Film Festival (SIFF)

Bailey Lauerman | Lincoln Marathon

LLOYD&CO | Oscar de la Renta

BOTTEGA VENETA

LLOYD&CO | Bottega Veneta

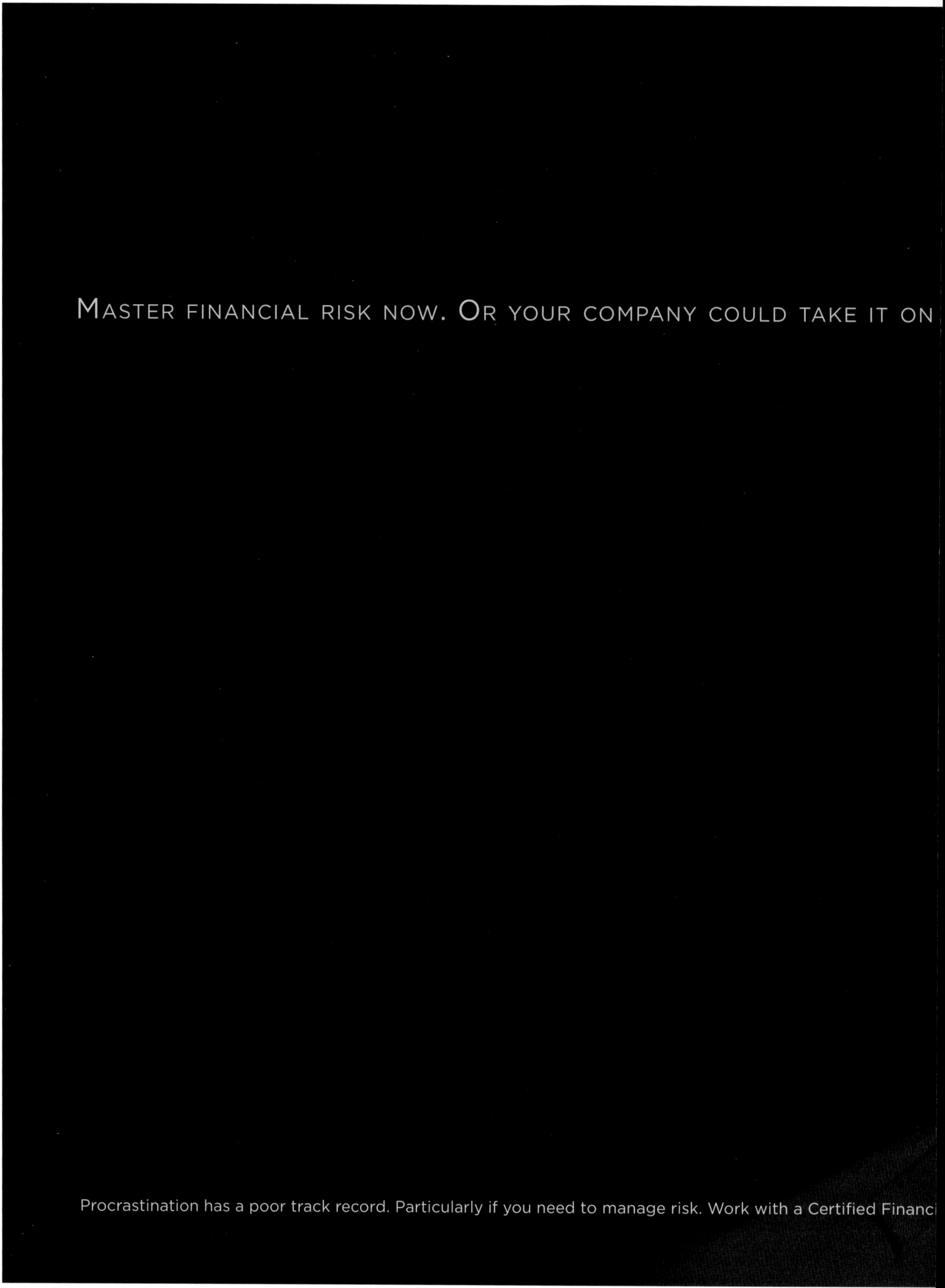

MASTER FINANCIAL RISK NOW. OR YOUR COMPANY COULD TAKE IT ON

Procrastination has a poor track record. Particularly if you need to manage risk. Work with a Certified Financi

E CHIN LATER.

sk Manager and catch problems before they turn nasty. Visit garp.org/frm.

FRM | Financial Risk Manager

THERE ISN'T A POT OF COPPER AT
THE END OF THE RAINBOW.

No one dreams of finding a pot that's filled with anything but gold. After all, it's the ultimate symbol of wealth.

Now it's more accessible than ever, thanks to SPDR Gold Shares. When you invest in GLD, you get a precise way to add gold to your portfolio. And you get an asset that offers diversification potential because it's generally not tied to the ups and downs of broad US equities.

So stop searching for a pot of gold and start investing in one. Visit spdrs.com/GLD for details.

SPDR GLD
GOLD SHARES

Precise in a world that isn't.

NO ONE EVER SAYS, "GO FOR THE SILVER!"

Athletes don't spend years in training just to have any old metal placed around their neck. They want the gold.

If you're an investor, you may feel the same way. With SPDR Gold Shares, it's now easier than ever. When you invest in GLD, you get a precise way to add gold to your portfolio. And you get an asset that offers diversification potential because it's generally not tied to the ups and downs of broad US equities.

If you believe gold is second to none, visit spdrs.com/GLD for details.

SPDR GLD
GOLD SHARES

Precise in a world that isn't.

YOU DON'T GET A TIN WATCH WHEN YOU RETIRE.

Everyone knows the best way to thank someone for a lifetime of service is with a gift made of gold.

Now it's more accessible than ever, thanks to SPDR Gold Shares. When you invest in GLD, you get a precise way to add gold to your portfolio. And you get an asset that offers diversification potential because it's generally not tied to the ups and downs of broad US equities.

A gold watch may be in your future. But a gold ETF is something you can have right now. Visit spdrs.com/GLD for details.

SPDR GLD
GOLD SHARES

Precise in a world that isn't.

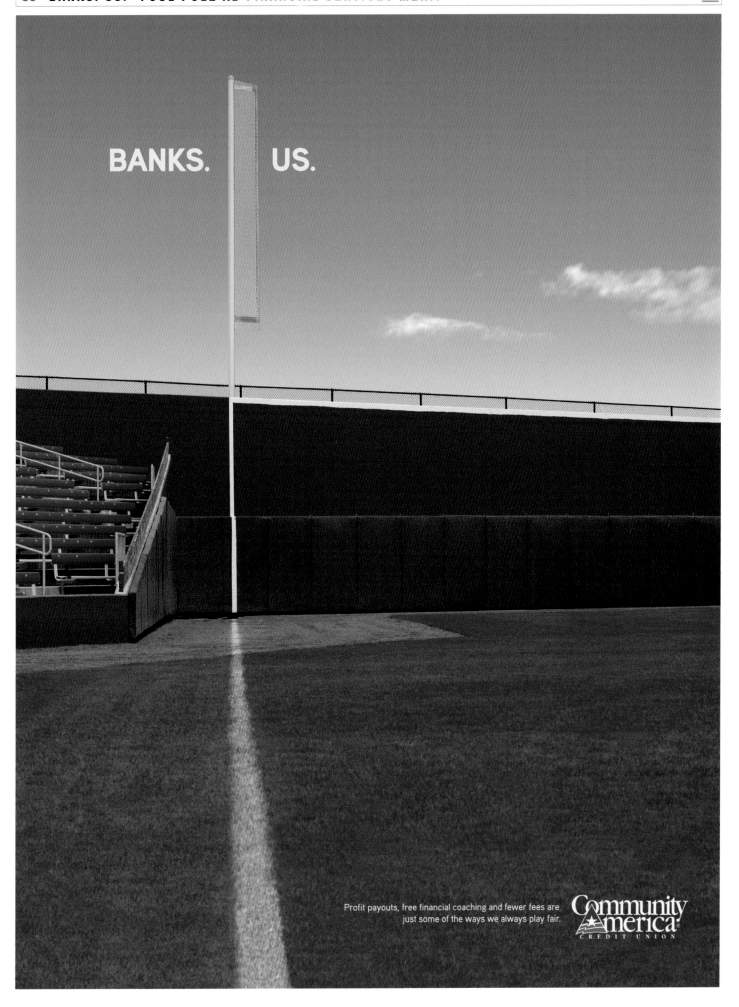

BANKS. US.

Profit payouts, free financial coaching and fewer fees are just some of the ways we always play fair.

BB AND MAPFRE INSURANCE GROUP

Don't text and drive.

IT'S AMAZING WHAT YOU CAN
PACK INTO A 12-OUNCE BOTTLE.
FOUNDERSBREWING.COM

IT'S AMAZING WHAT YOU CAN
PACK INTO A 12-OUNCE BOTTLE.

FOUNDERSBREWING.COM

FounderS
ALL DAY IPA
SESSION ALE

©2013 CytoSport, Inc. MUSCLEMILK.COM ⓊD

STRENGTH

TO JUMP HIGHER
O PLAY SMARTER
O OWN THE BOARDS
WIN

CHOCOLATE
NATURALLY AND ARTIFICIALLY FLAVORED

GENUINE

MUSCLE MILK

CONTAINS NO MILK
Includes Milk Proteins

PROTEIN NUTRITION SHAKE

230

WORKOUT RECOVERY FUEL

GIVE ME STRENGTH

TO PUSH HARDER
TO RUN FASTER
TO GO FURTHER

CHOCOLATE
NATURALLY AND ARTIFICIALLY FLAVORED

GENUINE

MUSCLE
MILK
LIGHT

CONTAINS NO MILK

Includes Milk Proteins

PROTEIN
NUTRITION
SHAKE

WORKOUT RECOVERY FUEL

©2013 CytoSport, Inc. **MUSCLEMILK.COM**

MATTY REED | Triathlete

GIVE ME STRENGTH

TO SWIM FASTER
TO BIKE STRONGER
TO RUN THROUGH THE WALL
TO WIN

CHOCOLATE
NATURALLY AND ARTIFICIALLY FLAVORED

GENUINE
MUSCLE
MILK®
CONTAINS NO MILK
Includes Milk Proteins
PROTEIN NUTRITION SHAKE

WORKOUT RECOVERY FUEL

©2013 CytoSport, Inc. MUSCLEMILK.COM

One Italian masterpiece deserves another.

It's Häagen-Dazs® precisely combined with a thousand years of Italian tradition. New Häagen-Dazs gelato. Inspired by Italy and *made like no other.*®

©HDIP, Inc.

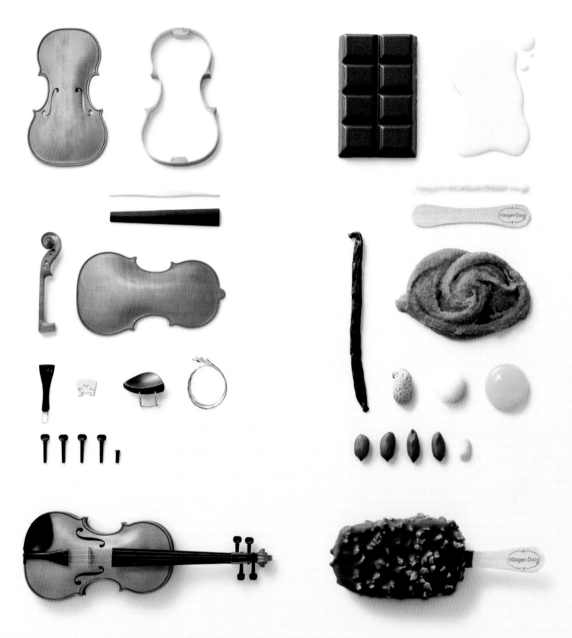

Precisely crafted to strike the perfect note.
First, we find the world's finest ingredients. Then, we mix them together until they sing. Häagen-Dazs® ice cream bars. Made like no other.®

★STAND WITH★ STILTON

ROQUEFORT ★THE VOTE!★

ROQUEFO

JOIN THE CHEESE PARTY

OCT
10

HAIL TO THE CHEESE

Central Market

OCT
23

JOIN THE CHEESE PARTY

OCT
10

HAIL TO THE CHEESE

Central Market

OCT
23

RBMM/The Richards Group | Central Market

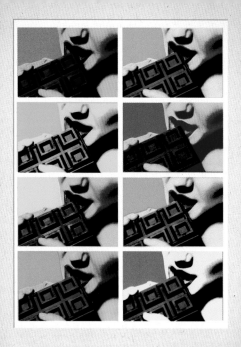

THE
CHOCOLATE COLLECTION
PRESENTED BY
CentralMarket
FEB 6 · FEB 14

THE
CHOCOLATE COLLECTION
PRESENTED BY
CentralMarket
FEB 6 · FEB 14

THE
CHOCOLATE COLLECTION
PRESENTED BY
CentralMarket
FEB 6 · FEB 14

THE
CHOCOLATE COLLECTION
PRESENTED BY
CentralMarket
FEB 6 · FEB 14

THE

CHOCOLATE COLLECTION

PRESENTED BY

Central Market
H·E·B

FEB
6

FEB
14

RBMM/The Richards Group | **Central Market**

¡ Sorpresa !

Populicom, Inc. | Pillsbury, B. Fernández & Hnos.

¿Qué celebras?

MY DARLING *WISCONSIN CHEESE*, YOU ARE MY SUN *AND* MY MOON. IF IT WEREN'T FOR YOUR ENDLESS LOVE *AND* DEVOTION. I WOULDN'T be the DELICIOUSLY LOVED PASTA THAT I AM TODAY.

You Complete Me.
~MACARONI

WISCONSIN CHEESE

Outdo Ordinary™
EatWisconsinCheese.com

MY BELOVED *WISCONSIN CHEESE*, I CAN HONESTLY SAY THAT I'M A BETTER HAM HAVING KNOWN YOU. WITHOUT YOUR SUPPORT *AND* COMPANIONSHIP I WOULDN'T be THE MEAT I AM TODAY.

Lovingly Yours,
~SMOKED HAM

WISCONSIN CHEESE

Outdo Ordinary™
EatWisconsinCheese.com

MY DEAREST WISCONSIN CHEESE, YOU ARE MY FRIEND. MY ROCK. YOU TURNED THIS ORDINARY SPUD INTO A SHINING STAR. YOU ELEVATED ME FROM A HUMBLE SIDEKICK TO "PLEASE PASS THE POTATOES."

Truly and Lovingly.
~POTATO

Outdo Ordinary™
EatWisconsinCheese.com

© 2013 Wisconsin Milk Marketing Board, Inc.

Some liqueurs are imported from foreign countries.

Others are smuggled out of crumbling empires.

Real Character

This is The House of Zwack
Experience real character in every bottle.

UNICUM † ZWACK † UNICUM PLUM

Please Drink Responsibly.
©2013 Imported by Diageo, Norwalk, CT.

No unauthorized ingredients were allowed in his recipes.

Including the Red Army.

Real Character

This is The House of Zwack

Experience real character in every bottle.

Please Drink Responsibly.
©2013 Imported by Diageo, Norwalk, CT.

BECAUSE NOT EVERYONE IS BORN WITH OOMPH.

PURE PREMIUM COCONUT WATER

NATURAL **OOMPH** FROM COCONUTS

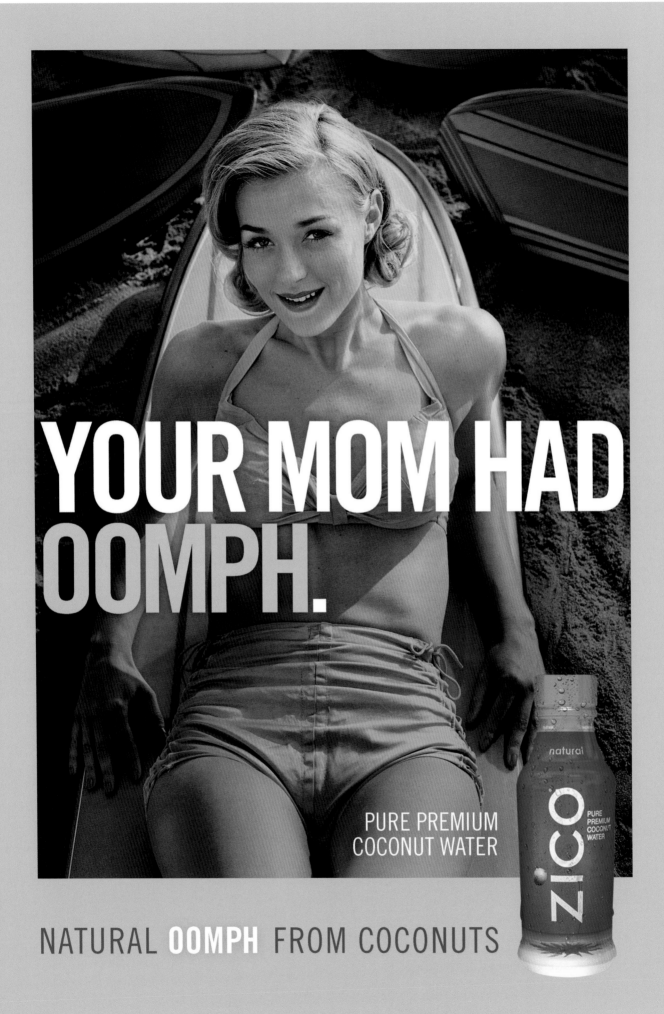

YOUR MOM HAD OOMPH.

PURE PREMIUM COCONUT WATER

NATURAL **OOMPH** FROM COCONUTS

UNLIKE WHOOP-ASS, OOMPH DOESN'T COME IN A CAN.

PURE PREMIUM
COCONUT WATER

NATURAL **OOMPH** FROM COCONUTS

ZICO
natural
ZICO
PURE
PREMIUM
COCONUT
WATER

Butler, Shine, Stern & Partners | ZICO Pure Premium Coconut Water

BRING THE FARM HOME.
PICKERING TOWN CENTRE
Farmers' Market
Tuesdays 11am - 6pm until October 15

Elixir | Pickering Town Centre

VOTE FOR KEITH

★ **2012** ★

A 'STONE IN EVERY HAND, A TACO IN EVERY POT.

GREAT BEER
GREAT RESPONSIBILITY

© 2012 COORS BREWING CO., GOLDEN, CO

WWW.VOTESTONE2012.COM

Saatchi & Saatchi, NY | Keystone Light

Zulu Alpha Kilo | Modelo Molson Imports L.P.

©2012 COORE FOUNDATION

Too often, young girls let other people shape the way they see themselves — if they get called something often enough, they start to believe it's true. But when a girl is educated, empowered, and whole, it transforms the way others see her. At our workshops, we provide a safe environment that encourages self-esteem, respect, and responsibility. So girls get a chance to develop their own sense of who they are and what they can become.

Help us grow sisterhood at
GIRLSRIGHTOFWAY.ORG

GROW SISTERHOOD

THERE'S SO MUCH MORE TO US THAN YOU THINK.

It's easy to underestimate a hospital as familiar as OU Medical Center Edmond. But behind our reputation for great care lies some of the area's most advanced technology. We're pioneering procedures like Oklahoma's first single-incision gallbladder removal using robotic surgery. And our digital technology is second to none. Which means we have the depth and expertise to bring you options you never imagined. Because we're big on exceeding expectations. **Read about our breakthrough gallbladder surgery at EdmondFirsts.com.**

Medical Center *Edmond*

HCA Health Services of Oklahoma, (d.b.a. OU Medical Center) is not part of, nor operated by, the University of Oklahoma.

life, liberty and the pursuit of :)

 When you need to take your tank from empty to happy, fill up on :) **fuel.**
It gives you a mobile place to store, gauge and share the things that fuel your
happy, whether it's a photo, song, place, video, sound, or thought. :) **fuel is
available at the iPhone App store or download it with the QR code.**

:) **fuel**™
fill up on happy.

MY GAL SAL

STAND EYE TO EYE WITH HISTORY.

ANDREW HIGGINS DR. BETWEEN CAMP AND MAGAZINE STREETS

ries of the moment.

o keep inflation under control and to
ess susceptible to shocks like sudden in-
cademic observers—including Fed chair-
2004 speech—have taken to calling this
ration." Instead of the sharp swings in
aracterized the U.S. before the 1980s,
oomlets and bustlets happening all the
es and different regions.

ir central bankers. For the rest of us it's
ou look at the economy today, it's meta-
thail, and the system can remain quite
y the CEO of Global Business Network.
ssing firm that evolved out of Royal
tho-planning operation. "You're not de-
nnection anymore. Anything that goes
in route around it pretty quickly." Partly
had a year of negative GDP growth since
o 1982). Pity those, however, who get
be it's meta-stable for every actor," says
less secure than it used to be."

hat is the perversity at work when we
lk in Fed-speak: Some of the very
ges that have made the Fed's job
er over the past quarter-century have
e our lives harder. Jobs are less secure,
enefits like health care and pensions
ess certain, than in the decades fol-
g World War II. That makes it far
er for workers to force pay raises and
asier for a central bank to keep in-
n in check. The Fed view of the world
quite as worker-unfriendly as it was
e mid-1990s, when the stock market
whenever the unemployment rate
up because that meant the Fed
dn't have to raise rates. But there's
omething strange about worrying
with Alan Greenspan whether the

100 YEARS OF

Picasso & Chicago

February 20 - May 12   *Valet parking now available*   **www.artic.edu/picasso**

Lead Corporate Sponsor: Major funding provided by   Annual support provided by the Exhibitions Trust: Goldman Sachs, Kenneth and
                                   the Auxiliary Board of the   Anne Griffin, Thomas and Margot Pritzker, the Earl and Brenda Shapiro Foundation,
BMO ● Harris Bank   Art Institute of Chicago.   the Trott Family Foundation, and the Woman's Board of the Art Institute of Chicago.

ART
INSTITVTE
CHICAGO

BE A VITAL PART OF THE PERFORMANCE. UP*A*F UNITEDPERFORMINGARTSFUND
Donate at www.UPAF.org.

© 2013 United Performing Arts Fund, Milwaukee, Wisconsin. All rights reserved. Trumpet: Alan Campbell, Milwaukee Symphony Orchestra

WHERE EVERY DOG'S A GENIUS   **CANINE COLLEGE**

(952) 922-5015

WHERE EVERY DOG'S A GENIUS CANINE COLLEGE

(952) 922-5015

BBDO Proximity Minneapolis | Canine College Training Center

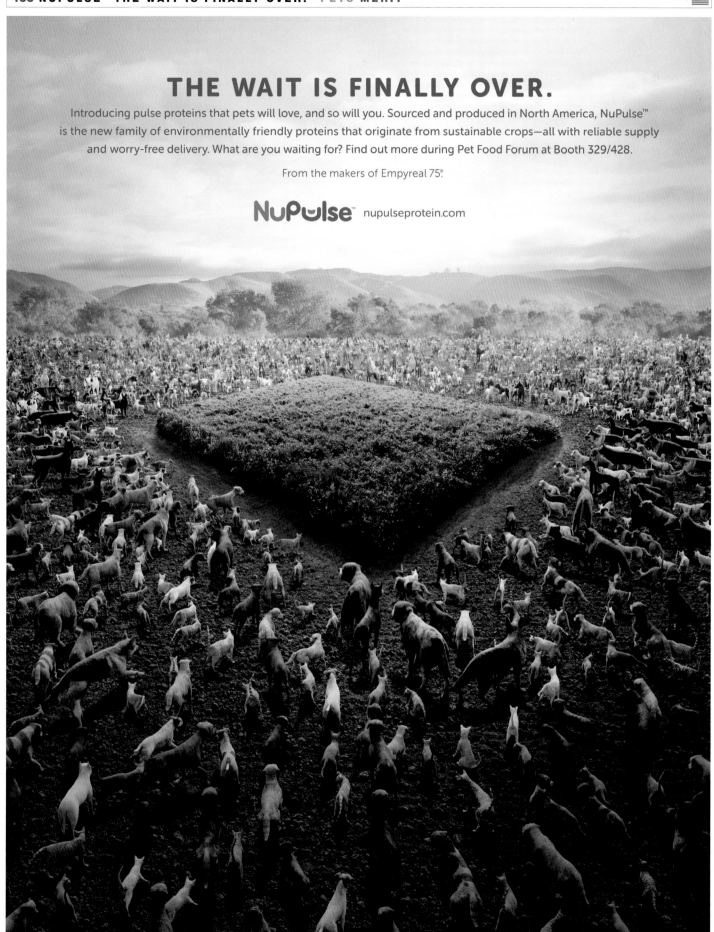

Bailey Lauerman | Cargill

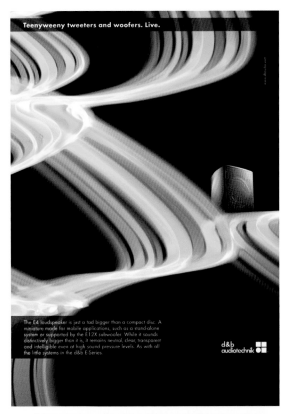

Teenyweeny tweeters and woofers. Live.

The E4 loudspeaker is just a tad bigger than a compact disc. A miniature made for mobile applications, such as a stand-alone system or supported by the E12X subwoofer. While it sounds distinctively bigger than it is, it remains neutral, clear, transparent and intelligible even at high sound pressure levels. As with all the little systems in the d&b E-Series.

d&b audiotechnik

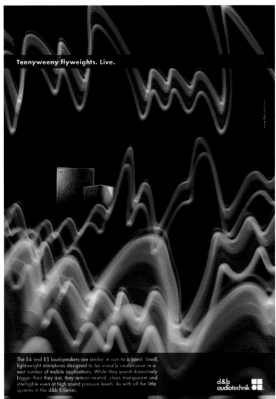

Teenyweeny flyweights. Live.

The E4 and E5 loudspeakers are similar in size to a hand. Small, lightweight miniatures designed to be visually unobtrusive in a vast number of mobile applications. While they sound distinctively bigger than they are, they remain neutral, clear, transparent and intelligible even at high sound pressure levels. As with all the little systems in the d&b E-Series.

d&b audiotechnik

Teenyweeny coaxial systems. Live.

The E4 and E5 loudspeakers are slightly bigger than a wallet. Efficient miniatures for mobile speech and music reinforcement, with up to four being driven by each channel of a d&b amplifier. While they sound distinctively bigger than they are, they remain neutral, clear, transparent and intelligible even at high sound pressure levels. As with all the little systems in the d&b E-Series.

d&b audiotechnik

Teenyweeny versatility. Live.

The E5 loudspeaker is probably the size of a paperback. A miniature, nevertheless, with a conically symmetric directivity. Intended for mobile applications such as delays, infills and surround sound. While it sounds distinctively bigger than it is, it remains neutral, clear, transparent and intelligible even at high sound pressure levels. As with all the little systems in the d&b E-Series.

d&b audiotechnik

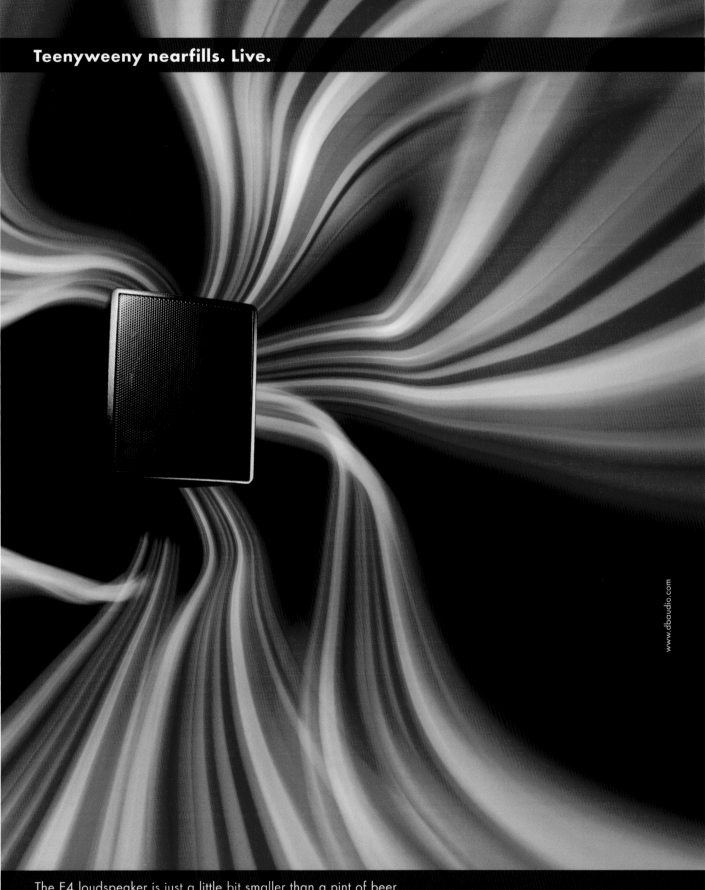

Teenyweeny nearfills. Live.

www.dbaudio.com

The E4 loudspeaker is just a little bit smaller than a pint of beer.
A coaxial built miniature, with a conically symmetric 100° directivity.
Made for even reinforcement in the near field, it can be mounted
in any orientation, and is almost invisible. While it sounds distinctively
bigger than it is, it remains neutral, clear, transparent and intelligible
even at high sound pressure levels. As with all the little systems
in the d&b E-Series.

d&b
audiotechnik

Schneider/Waibel I **d&b audiotechnik GmbH**

Don't let yesterday's breakfast ruin tonight's dessert.

Cleans dishes the first time.

Publicis Kaplan Thaler | P&G/ Cascade

Don't let tonight's dinner mess up tomorrow's dessert.

Cleans dishes the first time.

Don't let tonight's dinner mess up tomorrow's breakfast.

Cleans dishes the first time.

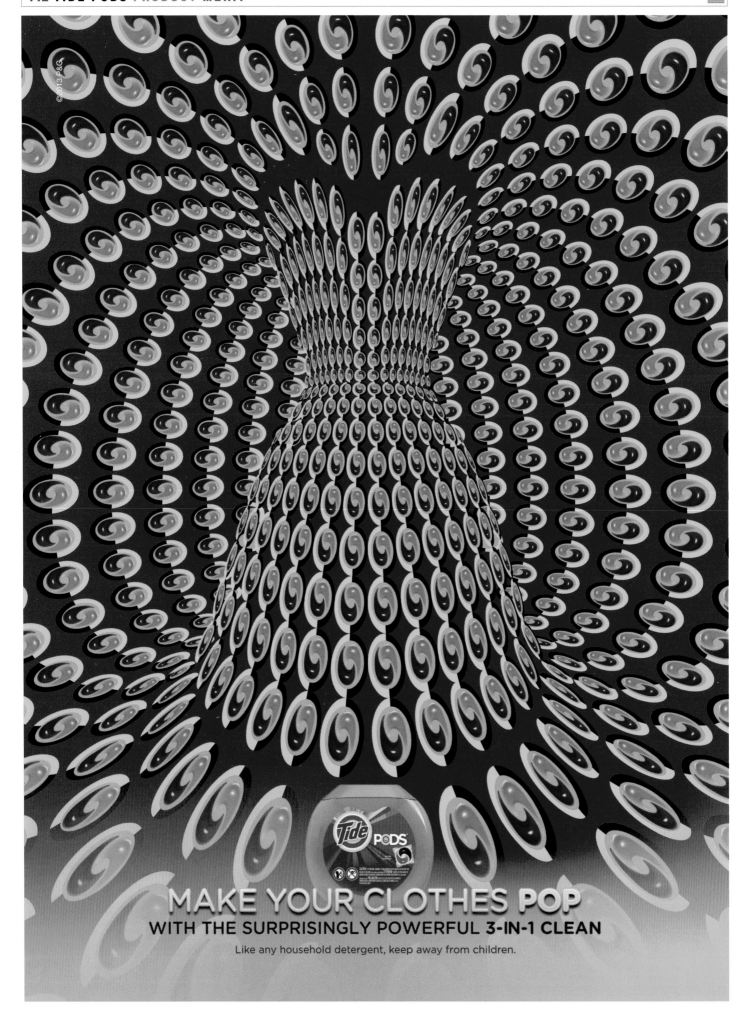

Get BreakFASTer.

Dries spills faster

© Procter & Gamble Inc., 2013

Introducing Wahl's new Hot-Cold Therapy line, featuring the only handheld massager with dual benefits. Cold helps relieve pain and decrease swelling. It's part of Wahl's full line of Hot-Cold Therapy products, which now includes Vibrating Therapeutic Gel Packs that help reduce muscle inflammation.

Always consult a physician with any questions you may have regarding a medical condition. © 2013 Wahl Clipper Corporation

WAHLMASSAGERS.COM

ICE AFTER.

HEAT BEFORE.

WAHLMASSAGERS.COM

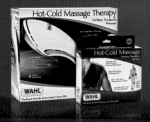

Introducing Wahl's new Hot-Cold Therapy line, featuring the only handheld massager with dual benefits. Heat helps relax muscles and increase blood flow. It's part of Wahl's full line of Hot-Cold Therapy products, which now includes Vibrating Therapeutic Gel Packs that help reduce muscle inflammation.

Always consult a physician with any questions you may have regarding a medical condition. © 2013 Wahl Clipper Corporation

WAHL
HOME PRODUCTS

" Look before you _____. "

According to *Canadian Lawyer's* recent survey, most corporate counsel will consider cost and value for money as deciding factors when evaluating outside firms, while *Inside Counsel* reports that many companies are looking to increase their use of regional firms for their high-quality legal work, prioritized personal service, and a "faster on their feet" approach.

WeirFoulds

Protect your future. Gain a **competitive** advantage. WeirFoulds LLP. 416.365.1110 www.weirfoulds.com

" Hold all the _____. "

You're ahead of the game when the cards are in your favour. Our litigators are the aces in your pack. That's why WeirFoulds is a "litigation firm through and through with a marvelous track record", *Chambers Global*.

WeirFoulds

Protect your future. Gain a **competitive** advantage. WeirFoulds LLP. 416.365.1110 www.weirfoulds.com

" More _____ for your buck. "

According to *Canadian Lawyer's* recent survey, most corporate counsel will consider cost and value for money as deciding factors when evaluating outside firms, while *Inside Counsel* reports that many companies are looking to increase their use of regional firms for their high-quality legal work, prioritized personal service, and a "faster on their feet" approach.

WeirFoulds

Protect your future. Gain a **competitive** advantage. WeirFoulds LLP. 416.365.1110 www.weirfoulds.com

" Take the _____ by the horns. "

We know wrangling a P3 project, regulatory matter or municipal management is no simple task. **Ranked in the Top 10 in Administrative and Public Law in Canada by** *Best Lawyers in Canada*, WeirFoulds is leading the way to get the job done - and all before you start seeing red.

WeirFoulds

Protect your future. Gain a **competitive** advantage. WeirFoulds LLP. 416.365.1110 www.weirfoulds.com

"More _____ for your buck."

According to *Canadian Lawyer's* recent survey, most corporate counsel will consider cost and value for money as deciding factors when evaluating outside firms, while *Inside Counsel* reports that many companies are looking to increase their use of regional firms for their high-quality legal work, prioritized personal service, and a "faster on their feet" approach.

WeirFoulds

Protect your future. Gain a **competitive** advantage. WeirFoulds LLP.

416.365.1110
www.weirfoulds.com

DECK THE HOLIDAYS

Observation Deck at Rockefeller Center®
50th Street between 5th and 6th Avenue
Open Daily from 8am to Midnight
212-698-2000 | topoftherocknyc.com
@rockcenternyc

TOP
OF THE
ROCK®

Pentagram Design | Tishman Speyer

DECK THE HOLIDAYS

Observation Deck at Rockefeller Center®
50th Street between 5th and 6th Avenue
Open Daily from 8am to Midnight
212-698-2000 | topoftherocknyc.com
@rockcenternyc

TOP
OF THE
ROCK®

DECK THE HOLIDAYS

Observation Deck at Rockefeller Center®
50th Street between 5th and 6th Avenue
Open Daily from 8am to Midnight
212-698-2000 | topoftherocknyc.com
@rockcenternyc

TOP
OF THE
ROCK®

DECK THE HOLIDAYS

Observation Deck at Rockefeller Center®
50th Street between 5th and 6th Avenue
Open Daily from 8am to Midnight
212-698-2000 | topoftherocknyc.com
@rockcenternyc

TOP
OF THE
ROCK®

DECK THE HOLIDAYS

Observation Deck at Rockefeller Center®
50th Street between 5th and 6th Avenue
Open Daily from 8am to Midnight
212-698-2000 | topoftherocknyc.com
@rockcenternyc

TOP
OF THE
ROCK®

THE PLAZA CAFÉ
AT ROCKEFELLER CENTER®

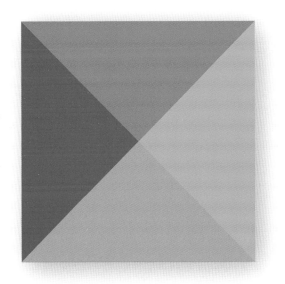
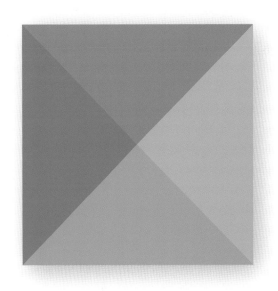
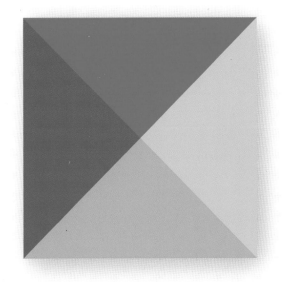
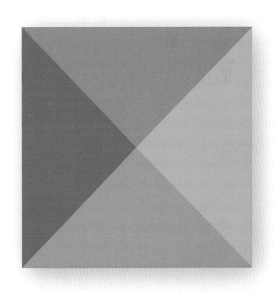

Monday–Saturday:
11:30am–10:00pm
Sunday:
11:30am–5:00pm

Rockefeller Center
212.632.3975
rockefellercenter.com
@rockcenternyc

You are fine.

Oh yeah. You are so fine, supermodels wish they were as fine as you.

You walk on air. It's like you came down from heaven. There's just no

other way to say it. You are fine. And when you get pregnant, you are

still going to be fine. Fine with all those trips to the doctor without

me. Fine with the morning sickness you are going to have, at home

all alone. Fine with the 12 hours of painful labor you're going to have

without me around to hold your hand. Fine with changing all those

dirty, nasty diapers. Fine with getting up in the middle of the night

when the baby is screaming to be fed. You are fine with the endless

hours of hard work it is to raise a child all by yourself. That's right

honey. There's no doubt in my mind. You are fine. Seriously. Fine.

Still think having a baby as a teen sounds like a good idea?

BabyCanWait.com

Baby, you're the one.

No seriously, honey, you're the one. You're the one, I just know it.

You're the one who's going to carry our baby. You're the one who's going to go to all those doctor appointments. You're the one who's going to go through all those intense hours of excruciating, painful labor. You're the one who's going to deal with those disgusting, dirty diapers. You're the one who's going to have to pull yourself out of bed at 3 in the morning because the baby is crying out to be fed. Yeah baby, you're the one. You're the one who's going to have to deal with the embarrassing public tantrums. You're the one who's going to have to find daycare so you can work to pay for all the stuff the baby needs. Yeah baby, you're the one.

Still think having a baby as a teen sounds like a good idea?

BabyCanWait.com

Serve | United Way of Greater Milwaukee

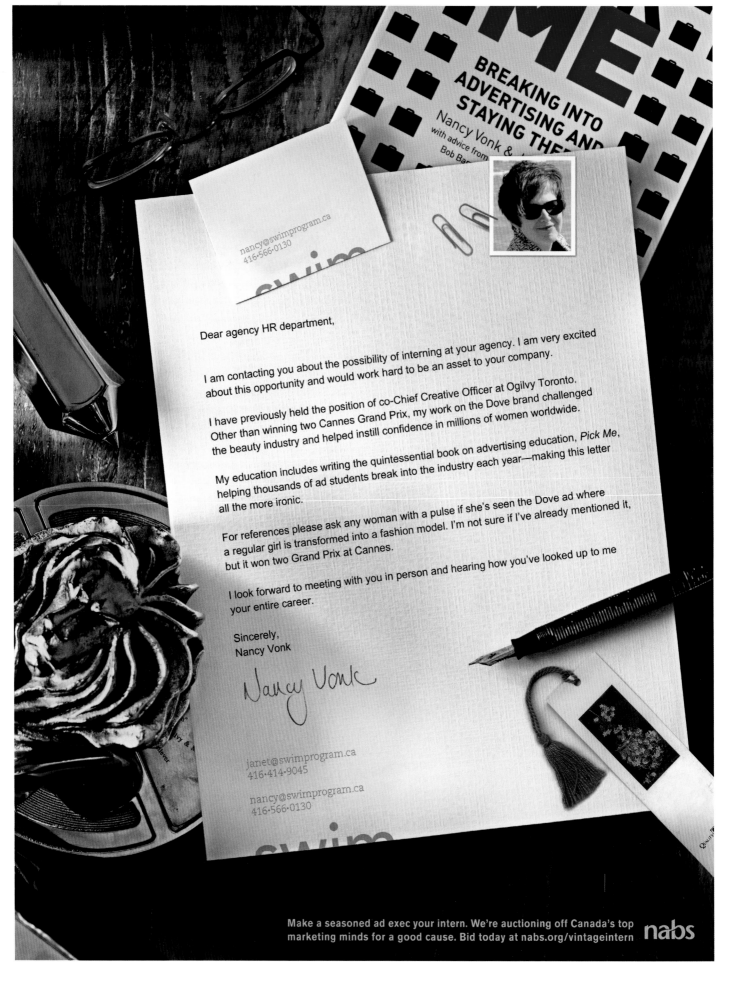

Dear agency HR department,

I am contacting you about the possibility of interning at your agency. I am very excited about this opportunity and would work hard to be an asset to your company.

I have previously held the position of co-Chief Creative Officer at Ogilvy Toronto. Other than winning two Cannes Grand Prix, my work on the Dove brand challenged the beauty industry and helped instill confidence in millions of women worldwide.

My education includes writing the quintessential book on advertising education, *Pick Me*, helping thousands of ad students break into the industry each year—making this letter all the more ironic.

For references please ask any woman with a pulse if she's seen the Dove ad where a regular girl is transformed into a fashion model. I'm not sure if I've already mentioned it, but it won two Grand Prix at Cannes.

I look forward to meeting with you in person and hearing how you've looked up to me your entire career.

Sincerely,
Nancy Vonk

Nancy Vonk

janet@swimprogram.ca
416·414·9045

nancy@swimprogram.ca
416·566·0130

Make a seasoned ad exec your intern. We're auctioning off Canada's top marketing minds for a good cause. Bid today at nabs.org/vintageintern **nabs**

Make a seasoned ad exec your intern. We're auctioning off Canada's top marketing minds for a good cause. Bid today at nabs.org/vintageintern

Spay or Neuter your pet before they become something you're not comfor

with. GreatPlainsSPCA.org

GREAT PLAINS SPCA
Be a hero.

Spay or Neuter your pet before they become something you're not comfortable with. GreatPlainsSPCA.org

GREAT PLAINS SPCA
Be a hero.

Spay or Neuter your pet before they become something you're not comfortable with. GreatPlainsSPCA.org

GREAT PLAINS SPCA
Be a hero.

Spay or Neuter your pet before they become something you're not comfortable with. GreatPlainsSPCA.org

GREAT PLAINS SPCA
Be a hero.

09/21/12

RECIPEACE

COME TOGETHER OVER FOOD

This Peace Day, September 21ST

Pledge for peace at *recipeaceday.org*

Leo Burnett | Peace One Day/D&AD

PEACE
ONE DAY

09/21/12

RECIPEACE

COME TOGETHER OVER FOOD
This Peace Day, September 21ST

Pledge for peace at *recipeaceday.org*

RECIPEACE

PEACE
ONE DAY

09/21/12

RECIPEACE

COME TOGETHER OVER FOOD

This Peace Day, September 21ST

Pledge for peace at *recipeaceday.org*

Leo Burnett | Peace One Day/D&AD

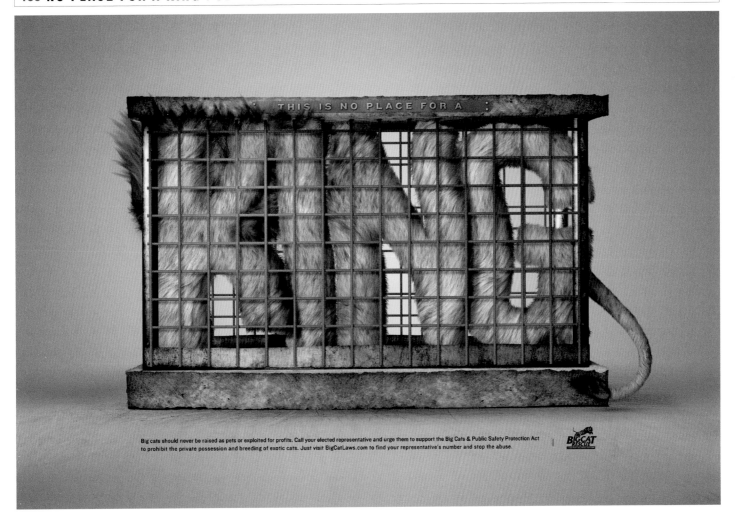

THINK YOUR TEEN LIFE WON'T CHANGE WITH A BABY?

BABYCANWAIT.COM

THINK YOUR TEEN LIFE WON'T CHANGE WITH A BABY?

BABYCANWAIT.COM

Our
national
blood
supply
is at
its
lowest
level
in 15
years.

Please
give
blood
now.

American
Red Cross

design for good.
A movement to ignite, accelerate and amplify
design-driven social change.

**American
Red Cross**

redcross.org

Our
national
blood
supply
is at
its
lowest
level
in 15
years.

Please
give
blood
now.

American
Red Cross

redcross.org

AIGA design for good.
A movement to ignite, accelerate and amplify
design-driven social change.

DEATH BY CHEESE GRATER.

This holiday, g

e gift of horror with a subscription to the world's #1 horror magazine. Fangoria.com FANGORIA

Zulu Alpha Kilo | **Fangoria Entertainment**

DEATH BY ROLLING PIN

This holiday, give the gift of horror with a subscription to the world's #1 horror magazine. Fangoria.com   FANGORIA

DEATH BY DECAF.

This holiday, give the gift of horror with a subscription to the world's #1 horror magazine. Fangoria.com   FANGORIA

DEATH BY TOASTER.

This holiday, give the gift of horror with a subscription to the world's #1 horror magazine. Fangoria.com   FANGORIA

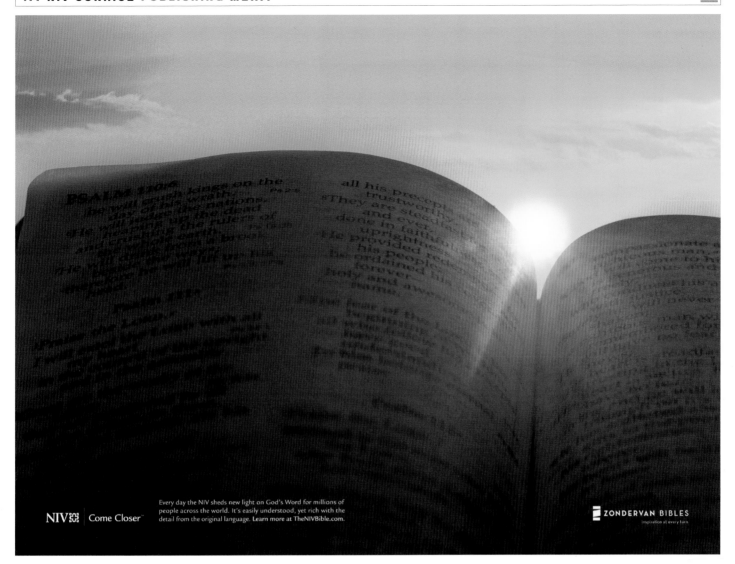

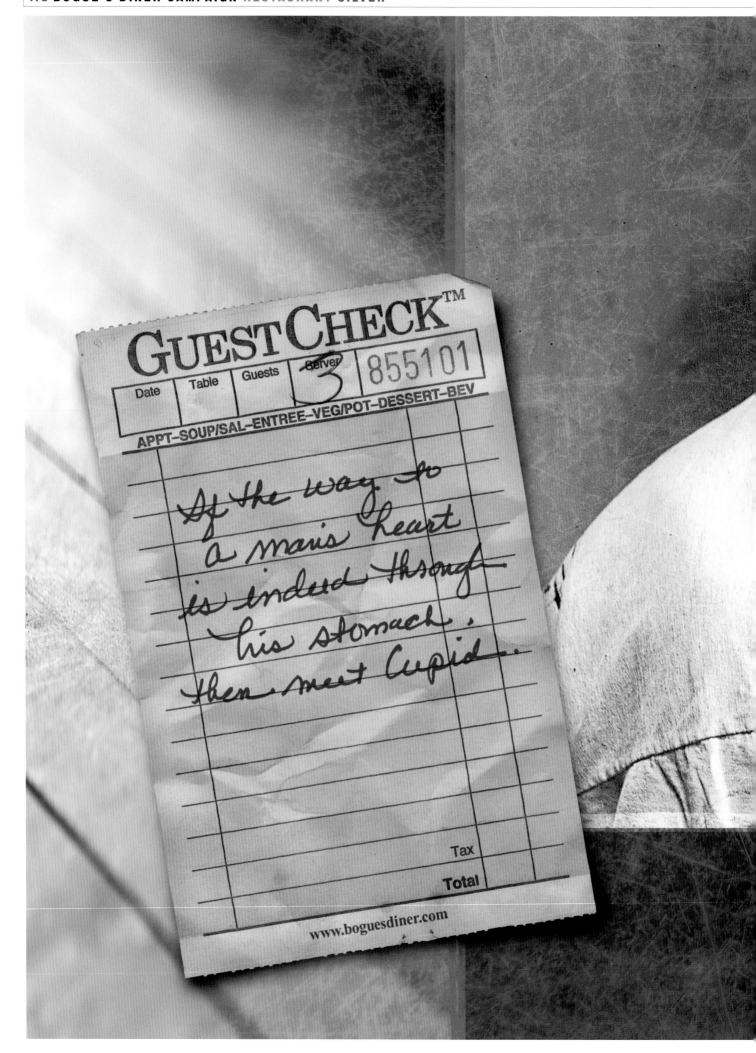

WHEN YOU'RE HUNGRY FOR WHAT'S REAL.

BOGUE'S
RESTAURANT

It's a religious experience.

Our Double Deck Cheeseburger is good.
Really good.

Big Boy

During our Grand Opening, we'll donate a portion of the proceeds from every Double Deck Cheeseburger® sold to benefit the Friendship Centers Of Emmet County Meals On Wheels program. Which is sure to leave everyone with a great feeling inside.

Ariel protective pre-wash makes laundry easy.

Ariel protective pre-wash makes laundry easy.

Beacon/Leo Burnett Tokyo | P&G Ariel

★ ★ ★ ★ ★ ★ ★ THE ★ ★ ★ ★ ★ ★ ★
FUTURE *is* BRIGHT
(don't forget the sunscreen)

Happy 4th of July from your friends at Peter Mayer.

THIS

IS NOT A FISHING POLE

IT'S A WEAPON

For one day, we grab our gear and do more than fish. We fight. All proceeds from the Yerrid Foundation's Grand Slam Celebrity Fishing Tournament go towards the Pediatric Cancer Foundation's mission to eradicate childhood cancer. PP+K is honored to be a part of the cause, and we won't rest until we wipe out this terrible disease. Together, we can create the biggest miracles for the littlest patients. So today, this isn't just a fishing pole. It's cancer's worst nightmare.

HELP SUPPORT THE FIGHT. VISIT FASTERCURE.ORG.

PP+K | PP+K

Proud supporter of the Grand Slam Celebrity Fishing Tournament, benefiting the Pediatric Cancer Foundation. | uniteppk.com

Michael Schwab Studio | James Whitburn, America's Cup 2013

You have to be born with big balls, too.

Footstock National Figure Eight Barefoot Waterski Championships
August 18-19, 2012 / Peshtigo Lake / Crandon, Wisconsin

Some are born with the heart of a champion. Others, the feet.

Her parents want her to be a doctor.
Nature wants something else entirely.

Footstock  National Figure Eight Barefoot Waterski Championships
August 18-19, 2012 / Peshtigo Lake / Crandon, Wisconsin

Footstock National Figure Eight Barefoot Waterski Championships
August 18-19, 2012 / Peshtigo Lake / Crandon, Wisconsin

SUPER NATURAL

The first, full line of all natural nutrition designed specifically for CrossFit athletes.
ALL NATURAL NUTRITION. SUPERNATURAL RESULTS. WFITNUTRITION.COM

SUPER
NATURAL

The first, full line of all natural nutrition designed specifically for CrossFit athletes.
ALL NATURAL NUTRITION. SUPERNATURAL RESULTS. WFITNUTRITION.COM

SUPER NATURAL

The first, full line of all natural nutrition designed specifically for CrossFit athletes.
ALL NATURAL NUTRITION. SUPERNATURAL RESULTS. WFITNUTRITION.COM

Wfit
Nutrition

Bold Worldwide | Weider Nutrition

IF
=EXTRAORDINARY=
CAME OVERNIGHT,

THEY'D CALL IT
ORDINARY.

HONOR THE GAME.

marucci
MarucciSports.com

Peter Mayer Advertising | Marucci Sports

BE A VITAL PART OF THE PERFORMANCE.

UNITEDPERFORMINGARTSFUND
Donate at www.UPAF.org.

© 2013 United Performing Arts Fund, Milwaukee, Wisconsin. All rights reserved. Dancer: Dani Kuepper, Danceworks, Inc.

Pentagram Design | Tishman Speyer

Where did you think cascarones came from?

Fiesta 2013 | 100+ Events | April 18-28 | VisitSanAntonio.com/Fiesta

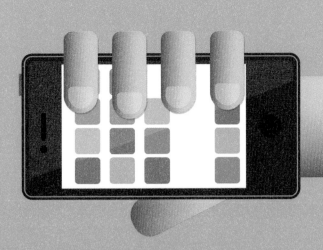

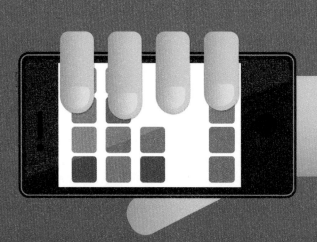

PRODUCTS   ENDORSERS   ABOUT   INFO

The closest  part to your soul.

©2012 Navarro Saxophone Mouthpieces | Website and creative by Mangos

Teaser billboard that ran for a week to arouse people's curiosity. On March 6th,

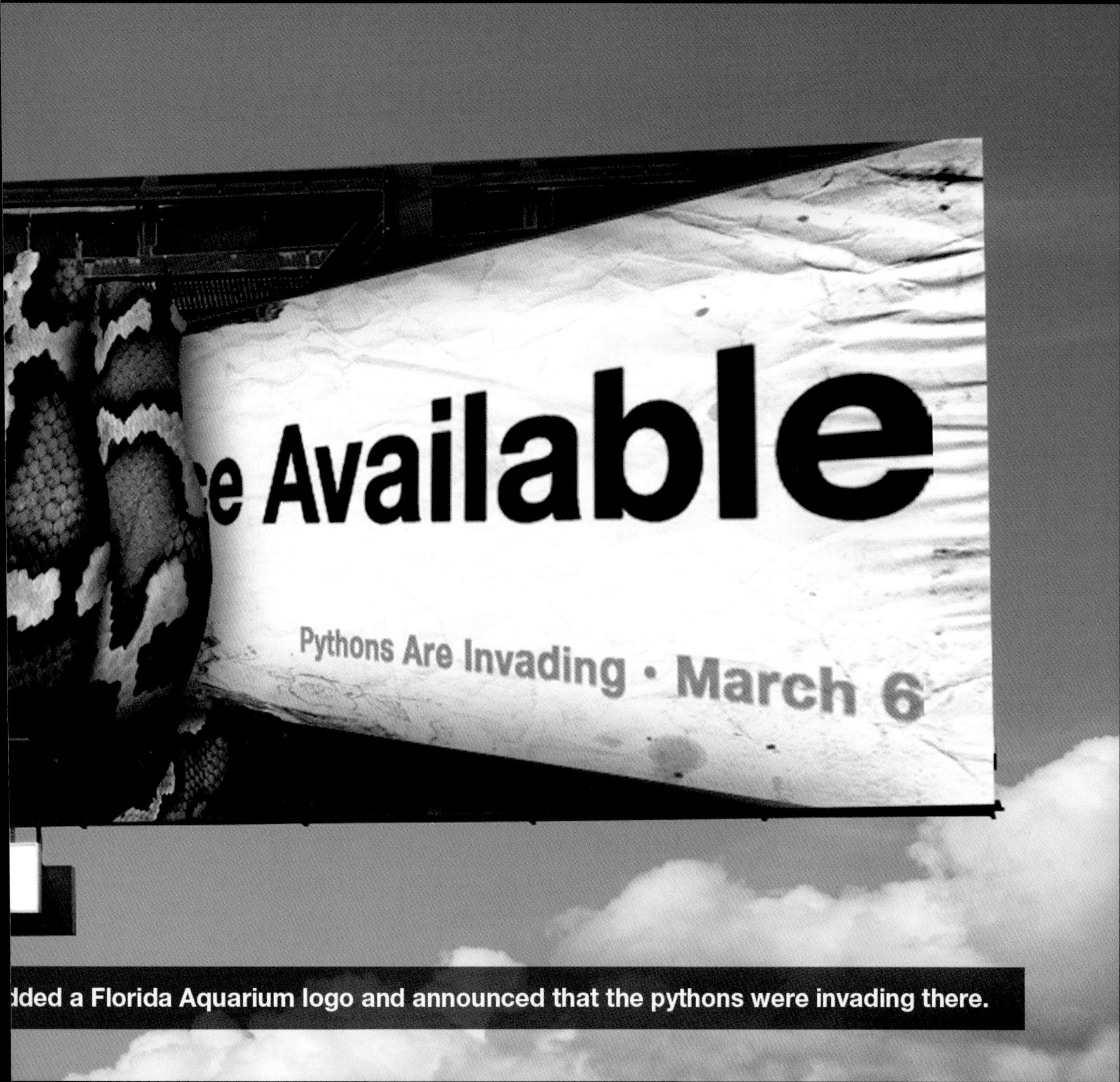

e Available

Pythons Are Invading • March 6

dded a Florida Aquarium logo and announced that the pythons were invading there.

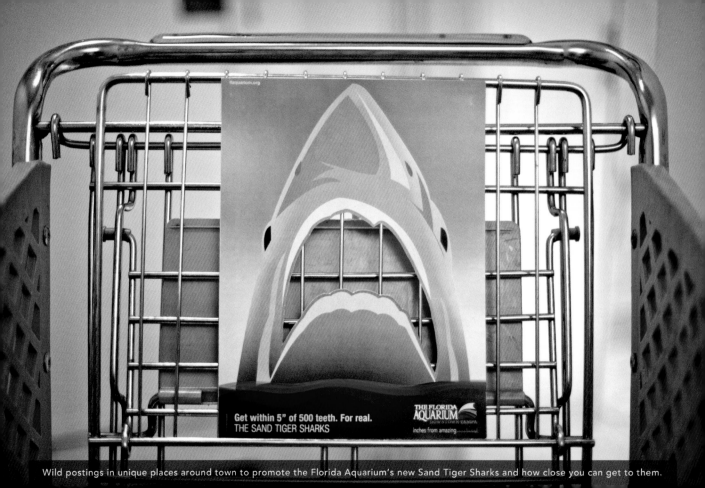

Get within 5" of 500 teeth. For real.
THE SAND TIGER SHARKS

THE FLORIDA
AQUARIUM
DOWNTOWN TAMPA

inches from amazing

Wild postings in unique places around town to promote the Florida Aquarium's new Sand Tiger Sharks and how close you can get to them.

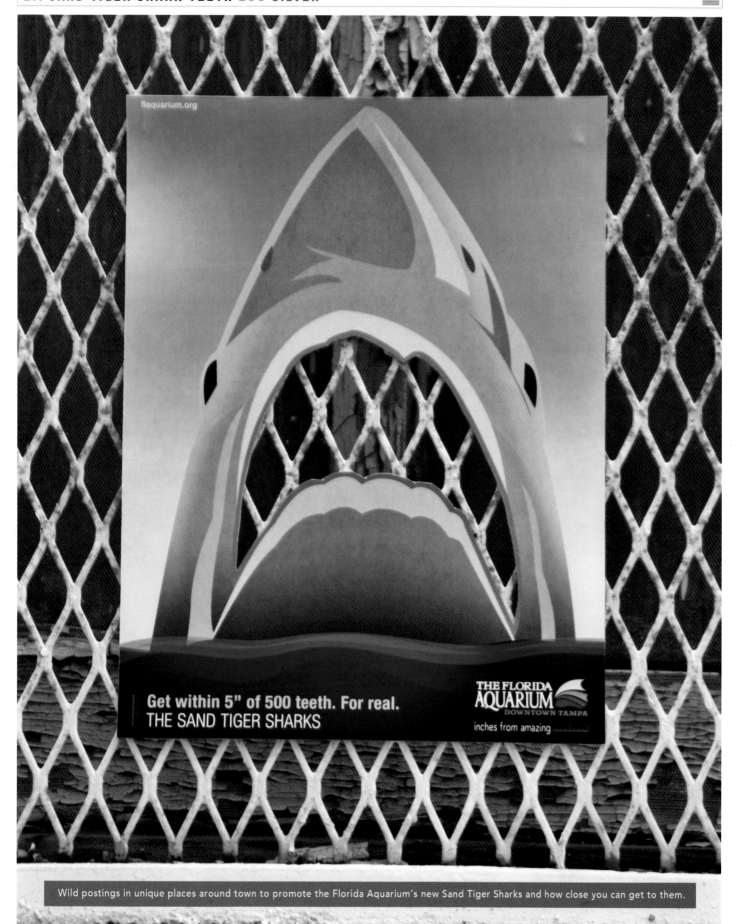

Wild postings in unique places around town to promote the Florida Aquarium's new Sand Tiger Sharks and how close you can get to them.

flaquarium.org

Get within 5" of 500 teeth. For re
THE SAND TIGER SHARKS

flaquarium.org

Wild postings in unique places around town to promote the Florida

arium's new Sand Tiger Sharks and how close you can get to them.

NOT
NOR
MAL

Butler, Shine, Stern & Partners | **MINI Global**

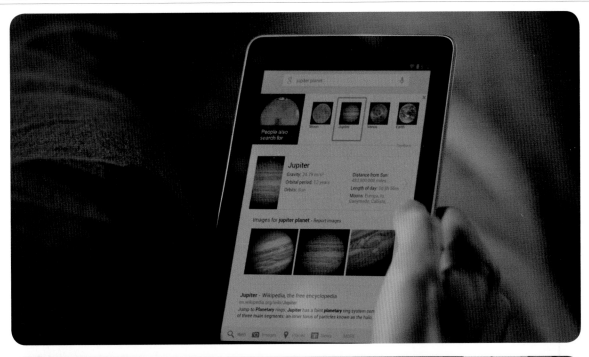

Butler, Shine, Stern & Partners | Google

OOMPH

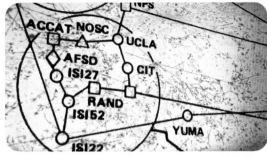

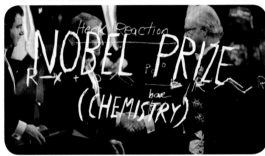

160over90 | UCLA

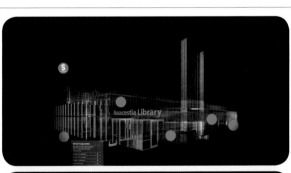

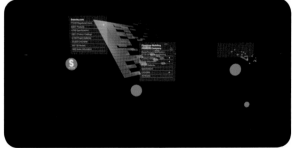

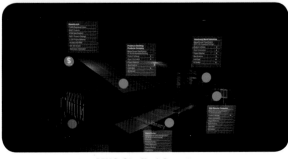

MHC Studio | Sweets

Butler, Shine, Stern & Partners | Isis

Saatchi & Saatchi, NY | Fruit Snacks

Credits & Commentary

16 TOYOTA AVALON 2013 | Ad Agency: Saatchi & Saatchi, LA
Creative Director: John Payne | Associate Creative Director: Jera Mehrdad
Associate Creative Director: Matthew Poitras | Art Directors: Erek Vinluan,
Max Wang | Retoucher: Rebecca Manson | Copywriters: Ben George, Matthew Poitras
Photography Studio: Christopher Griffith Studios | Client: Toyota Avalon

Assignment: The 2013 Avalon was a complete redesign. The campaign concept was to create an artistic interpretation of a vehicle being formed from a nondescript organic origin. Effectively, from nothing, came the new Avalon.

Approach: The challenge was to have the material that flows around and behind the vehicle be accurate to how it physically interacts with the shape of the vehicle. To do this, a scaled model of the car was created, painted matt grey. The model was then suspended in 5x5x8 feet water tanks at angles that were exact to hero angles previously shot on the car. Then a variety of materials were dropped onto areas of the model car in water, capturing varying interactions with the model. The model was then replaced with the actual car images, resulting in images that, although composited, are completely accurate in spacial association of the car to that which appears to emerge.

20 MPG / SUSPENSION / GRILLE | Ad Agency: The Richards Group
Creative Directors: Rob Baker, Jimmy Bonner | Art Director: Kellyn McGarity
Copywriter: Sue Batterton | Photographer: Matthew Turley | Client: Ram

24 OUTDOORSMAN | Ad Agency: The Richards Group | Creative Directors: Rob Baker,
Jimmy Bonner | Art Director: Justin McCormick | Copywriter: Rob Baker
Photographer: Matthew Turley | Client: Ram

29 CRAFTSMANSHIP / INSPIRATION / VERSATILITY | Ad Agency: The Richards Group
Creative Designers: Rob Baker, Jimmy Bonner | Art Directors: Mike LaTour
Copywriter: Chad Berry | Client: Ram

32 IRRESISTIBLE | Ad Agency: Charit Art | Designer: Charit Pusiri | Client: Amarit Co.,Ltd.

Assignment: The goal of this project is to illuminate the beautiful lines of the car, while also conveying the sense of being an open top roadster. We wanted the ad to be clean, yet sophisticated.

Approach: First we analyzed the goals which are mainly to create an ad that clearly depicts the car's beautiful shapes and its open top feel, combined with making the ads feel clean, but with a little gimmick and story to it to get the viewers' attention. So we came up with the concept of "Irresistible," in which we present the car in a clean, modern, open environment, in a contemporary style building with a swimming pool and some trees. The car is parked in the middle of the swimming pool on a concrete platform. These elements convey an unusual open parking space that the owner of the car has created to park his/her car in order to prevent him/her from driving it, the car being so 'irresistible' to drive.

34 TIFFIN MOTORHOMES "TICKETS" CAMPAIGN | Ad Agency: Lewis Communications
Executive Creative Director: Spencer Till | Creative Director/Art Director: Jason Bickell
Copywriter: Stephen Curry | Associate Creative Director: Roy Burns
Production Artist: Andy Cargile | Production Planner: Leigh Ann Motley
Client: Tiffin Motorhomes

Assignment: When you are selling RVs, it's very easy to get caught up in descriptions of individual specs and features. But during our decade of work for this Red Bay, Alabama-based RV manufacturer, we've sought to avoid that, instead using compelling lifestyle visuals to position the brand as an industry leader. Our assignment this year was to position Tiffin ownership as a rewarding, carefree experience.

Approach: Every person who buys a Tiffin has somewhere different they want to go, and a different idea of what the perfect escape may be. That individual freedom is at the very heart of the RV experience. For this campaign, we used imaginatively-worded tickets to bring to life the kind of distinctive, individual freedom that owning a Tiffin offers you.

37 TEST DRIVE TAKE DOWN - SPRING SALES EVENT "POSTERS"
Ad Agency: Butler, Shine, Stern & Partners | Creative Directors: Steve Mapp, Lyle Yetman
Art Director: Sinan Dagli | Copywriter: Bem Jimmerson | Client: MINI USA

Assignment: Celebrate MINI's 10 years in America by inviting customers to see what has made MINI the biggest small car in the U.S. Develop a test-drive program at the dealer level that is executed unlike any in the industry. It should be uniquely MINI, fun and smile-inducing.

Approach: After 10 years in America, MINI has proven that they are champions of the automotive arena. And they didn't get there by backing down from a little scuffle. So, we'll match up MINI with its closest competitors in a wrestling-style test drive battle and let folks decide for themselves who's champ. Each MINI model will take on a wrestling alter ego. We'll provide dealers with wrestling themed items, including posters, t-shirts, trading cards and challenger booklets. On the day of the main event, we'll provide wrestling ropes, retractable banners and even a title belt. All drivers who complete the Test Drive Takedown will be crowned champion and have the opportunity to acquire the ultimate trophy: a MINI of their own.

Results: MINI dealers embraced and got behind this theme, carrying out exciting events all over the country. Overall monthly sales hit a record high. During the MINI Test Drive Take Down campaign, MINI sold 2,309 cars alone. This was a 50 percent YOY increase for the month of April. Over 6,414 people attended the events and 24,000 people visited the MINIUSA.com event landing page during the campaign period.

39 THIS IS AMERICA | Ad Agency: Goodby Silverstein & Partners
Executive Creative Director: Ralph Watson | Art Director: Joe Albert
Copywriter: Jason Turner | Client: Chevrolet - Corvette

41 SAAB ORG CHART | Ad Agency: McCann Detroit | Creative Director: Matt Canzano
Art Director: Robin Chrumka | Copywriter: Mike Stocker | Client: Saab

Assignment: In a world where cars try to be all things to all people, Saab builds cars for only one type of driver: the serious driving enthusiast. Our objective was to communicate that in a clear and unique way.

Approach: Saabs have always stood apart from other vehicles on the road because Saab as a company was different. To illustrate this fact, we used the ultimate example of what's wrong with other car companies: the heavily hierarchical and layered organization that kills automotive purity. Then we twisted it to prove our point and put the Test Driver on top of the org chart.

Results: Some of the most fanatical Saab owners are those that work at Saab. After it ran, this ad was displayed in the offices of many Saab employees. The results were never measured because, soon after it broke, patent restrictions and legal battles ultimately crippled the company.

42 HOURGLASS | Ad Agency: PP+K | Executive Creative Director: Tom Kenney
Creative Director: Michael Schillig | Copywriter: Nick McMurdy | Art Director: Javier Quintana
Client: Tires Plus

Assignment: Tires Plus recently unveiled their new 59-Minute Quick Tire Install service, where they will install your tires in under an hour with an appointment, guaranteed. Our assignment was to create an in-store poster that would clearly and uniquely communicate this new service to current customers, mainly at the point of sale. The client wanted a graphic solution that could be utilized in many different communications pieces in the future.

Approach: Our approach was to focus on the "under an hour" differentiator that makes this service truly unique and marketable. Visually, we felt that an hourglass was the quickest "get" as far as demonstrating 60 minutes of time. After settling on the hourglass image, we then figured that the best way to communicate this entire service in one visual was to literally show a tire being built by the sands of the hourglass. So the single-minded selling proposition that the consumer takes away from this piece is that tires are completed in one hour's time.

Results: Our poster was highly received by the client. So much so, that we are actually beginning to utilize the tire hourglass image in other consumer communications pieces that will hit the market soon. We actually just finished a direct mail piece targeting first-time customers and we are using the hourglass creative to educate them on our 59-Minute Quick Tire Install service. When it's all said and done, we expect to get a lot of mileage (some pun intended) out of this creative.

43 BEEHIVE TIRE | Ad Agency: PP+K | Executive Creative Director: Tom Kenney
Creative Director: Michael Schillig | Copywriter: Michael Schillig
Art Director: Trushar Patel | Client: Tires Plus

Assignment: To create an in-store poster for Tires Plus that would emphasize the environmentally friendly traits of the Ecopia Tire in a very fresh and interesting way. We wanted to get people inquiring about the benefits of these tires and their powerful impact on fuel savings and the environment.

Approach: With all the competing messages for tires out there, we felt like we needed to do something really distinctive and highly impactful to get customers' attention and leave them with a memorable impression of the Ecopia Tire at Tires Plus. So we created the beehive tire image with some supporting copy that focused on its eco-friendly qualities — traits that we felt could naturally attract a "swarm" of bees and consumers.

Results: This powerful, visual-driven poster was well received by the client and became a conversation starter at the point of sale for these environmentally friendly Ecopia Tires. In fact, the poster was so well liked by Tires Plus that they requested a copy to hang up in their corporate offices.

44 AS NATURE INTENDED | Ad Agency: Publicis Kaplan Thaler
Chief Creative Officer: Rob Feakins | Executive Creative Director: David Corr
Copywriter: Lori Korchek | Art Director: Alessandra Melo | Client: P&G/Crest 3D White Strips

Assignment: Our job was to demonstrate the unprecedented level of whitening power of Crest 3-D Whitestrips Professional Effects. But what does the promise of whitening teeth as well as a professional really mean? It means Crest 3-D Whitestrips Professional Effects gives us the power to remove the effluence of years of excess more easily than ever before, revealing the smile we were born with, the smile that nature intended.

Approach: The smile that nature intended. We needed more than a page of pearly whites to communicate the effect of this new level of whitening power. Why not the ultimate product demo? A "before and after" that works in reverse? Nature polluted becomes nature restored. The absolute worst we can do to ourselves is reversed simply and easily to reveal a state of absolute perfection that was there all along.

Results: The clients were very pleased with the finished product. They felt the campaign elevated the purpose of professional whitening beyond vanity to something more meaningful: that Crest 3-D Whitestrips Professional Effects gives us the power to care for and appreciate the natural beauty we were all born with.

47 GLAMURE | Ad Agency: omdr Co., Ltd. | Creative Director: Osamu Misawa
Art Director: Osamu Misawa | Designer: Tasuku Matsumura
Photographer: Naohiro Tsukada | Client: MTG Co.,LTD

Assignment: This roll-on serum is formulated with highly concentrated placenta, which moisturizes and brightens the delicate eye area, creating more youthful looking skin. It has a unique, original function and method. Through this advertisement, we sought to communicate to customers that this product is made by the convergence of science technology and basic, natural ingredients.

Approach: Our client's development of this product spawned from two ideas: The power of nature and technology. The best way to truly utilize ingredients from nature is through the use of a "roll-on" applicator, designed by with those two ideas in mind. We wanted to express "Merging Natural Power with Science Technology Together" by visual communication.

Results: Our clients and customers were enthused by our cutting-edge advertisement of beauty tools, which uses the most advanced science and technology to bring something new to the world of cosmetics.

49 COURAGE ENCOURAGED | Ad Agency: Publicis Kaplan Thaler
Chief Creative Officer: Rob Feakins | Executive Creative Director: David Corr
Art Director: Einav Jacubovich | Copywriter: Todd Perelmuter
Photographer: Jason Nocito | Client: P&G/ Scope

Assignment: Our objective was to create a print campaign that would re-brand Scope Mouthwash and make it a relevant brand for millenials. The problem was that mouthwashes have always advertised like an oral care brand; talking about germs, garlic and onions — things no one, especially young people, want to talk about.

Approach: We stopped talking about bad breath and started talking about why people really use Scope Mouthwash — for the courage and confidence to make real human connections face-to-face.

Results: When the new print campaign hit the stands, people noticed. On Facebook, our fans grew from 170,000 people to 848,000 and it became one of the most talked about brands on Facebook. And we never spoke about garlic or onions again.

51 FAITH RADIO POSTER | Ad Agency: BRIGHT RED\TBWA
Executive Creative Director: Rob Kerr | Copywriter: Rob Kerr | Art Director: John Herd
Photographer: Stock | Client: Faith Radio

Assignment: Develop a cost-effective poster that can be placed on church bulletin boards to increase listeners to this Christian radio station.

Approach: Knowing that the client had little to no budget, we focused on a simple, yet powerful visual. All imagery was Royalty Free stock, proving that you don't need a huge budget to deliver great work.

52 DODGE - 6 WAYS | Ad Agency: MHC Studio | Chief Creative Officer: William Taylor
Art Director: Jason Scuderi | Designer: Jonathan Winn | Copy Strategy: Keith Fox
Marketing Strategy: Linda Brennan, Brenda Griffin, Eileen Lamadore, Elizabeth Schulson
Client: McGraw Hill Construction

Assignment: As the leading supplier of building project data and analytics to the architectural, engineering and construction industries, Dodge is well known but not well understood. So we developed a campaign built around our six customer benefit-oriented capabilities to define and clarify our services, build our brand and increase our market share.

Approach: The list of capabilities were developed by our leadership team, carefully vetted and infused throughout the organization, including training for our sales teams. We felt six is an interesting number for a manifesto because it was obviously thoughtfully developed or it would be a more typically numbered list, like 10 or five. We used the number six as a powerful mnemonic, giving us a firm foundation to build on our communications, explaining in clear terms how our complex analytics benefited our customers.

54 DODGE DOCUPRO | Ad Agency: MHC Studio | Chief Creative Officer: William Taylor
Art Director: Jonathan Winn | Designer: Jason Scuderi | Illustrator: Jason Scuderi
Copywriters: Dean Noble, Jonathan Winn, Karen Mcintyre | Marketing Strategy: Sue Peterson
Client: McGraw Hill Construction

Assignment: The Holy Grail of construction project management is control. There are plenty of products out there to help project managers manage time and costs, but DocuPro focuses on documents — which gives us an edge.

Approach: Collecting and updating construction documents is Dodge's primary business. DocuPro is an add-on product that organizes and disseminates those documents to all relevant stakeholders so document management is seamless. We leveraged that strength by re-framing the issue as control vs. chaos with an ad that shows a building as a series of documents. Our headline "Control the Documents. Control the Project." resonates with customers who know how often documents are updated — and who understand how important it is to keep everyone on the same page.

55 BEING ACCEPTED | Ad Agency: MacLaren McCann | Creative Directors: Sean Davison,
Mike Halminen | Group Creative Directors: Cam Boyd, Troy McGuinness
Art Director: Isabelle Santiago | Copywriter: Aaron Woolfson | Client: MasterCard

Assignment: MasterCard Canada created this timely ad to celebrate both Toronto Pride Week and the US Supreme Court ruling on the DOMA.

56 THE SWAN | Ad Agency: Ice House Design | Creative Director: Jack Owen
Senior Designer: Les Abraham | Photographer: Simon Plant
Client: Ian & Helen Wilmshurst. King's School, Bruton

Assignment: The environment in which British independent schools operate is competitive. However, we and our client believed there was scope to move away from the more traditional school advertising approach, thus providing us with the necessary 'cut through'. The recent (and excellent) ISI report the school had received gave us great copy; we felt these written messages were stronger and had more integrity than a conventional headline. As a consequence, the narrative within the image we were to create should be subtle and self-contained, without the necessity for a further line.

Approach: Our ambition was to create a single, strong image which, while elegant, was intriguing and had a suggestion of the 'King's' name within. Swans have a natural unification of grace and power as well as a significant royal connection. While investigating the swan approach it became appar-

ent that the 'taking flight' message was particularly appropriate for a high quality educational institution. The ethereal quality of the image was built using a variety of images including shots of the Somerset levels, the dovecote in Bruton and of course the bird, skies and splashes.

Results: The client was delighted with the concept and design on initial presentation of the campaign and this has been further positively reinforced with a 25 percent increase in admissions for 2013 and a significantly greater percentage for 2014.

58 BAYLOR MUSEUM CAMPAIGN | Ad Agency: Proof Advertising
Creative Director/Art Director: Craig Mikes | Copywriter: Dave Pernell
Photographer: Paul Swen | Client: Baylor University

Assignment: In the 10 years we have worked with Baylor, they have gone from declining applications to record admissions. From limited research to a nationally ranked research institution. And from the back of the Big 12 to the home of a Heisman trophy winner and leading the NCAA with the most wins across the major sports. But Baylor is more than just a university. The Baylor system also encompasses a hospital and health care system in Dallas, a medical college in Houston, a law school, a women's college and more. Few people know the full scope, but when they do, it enhances the perception of the school and all the related institutions. This campaign weaves together the full Baylor story by assembling the proud moments from each institution into a virtual Baylor museum. It unites all of them under a shared past and a shared vision for the future.

Approach: To tell the many milestones of Baylor history with authentic objects that allow as to highlight the varied stories. We wanted give a printed tour of our hero objects as if you were walking through a museum. The trick was to position and shoot each object at the same angle, lighting and position so the museum plaque and object was always in the same spot in each ad.

Results: The campaign was overwhelmingly embraced by supporters of all Baylor institutions. Unsolicited calls and emails praising the campaign came from alumni and board members alike. Baylor topped $100 million in donations each for two separate fundraising efforts — a record achievement.

60 ARCHITECTURAL RECORD CEU APP CAMPAIGN | Ad Agency: MHC Studio
Chief Creative Officer: William Taylor | Art Director: Jason Scuderi
Publisher: Laura Viscusi | Client: Architectural Record

Assignment: Architects and engineers must keep earning Continuing Education Units to maintain their licenses — quite a challenge, given their demanding schedules. So Architectural Record decided to make things easier, by developing the first CEU app that works offline.

Approach: No Wi-Fi? No problem. We appeal to time-crunched architects and engineers by showing how they can earn our Continuing Education Units on airplanes, in parks — anywhere they have a free hour.

Results: Thousands of architects and engineers have downloaded our app, keeping us at the leading edge of continuing education for the industry. To date, over 27,000 architects and design professionals have earned CE credits with us. In the 15 years we've been offering courses, we've awarded more than one million learning units!

62 ONE MILLION DEGREES INVITATION | Ad Agency: Leo Burnett
Design Director: Alisa Wolfson | Designer: Yoshi Minami | Copywriter: Jake Bogoch
Producer: Richard Blanco | Client: One Million Degrees

Assignment: One Million Degrees, a non-profit scholarship charity like none other, was hosting its largest fundraiser of the year: a food and wine tasting. Our assignment was to raise awareness of the event and create an invitation to drive ticket sales to the event.

Approach: We had to raise awareness of the event and create an invitation. Our approach was to do both, and simultaneously. Our solution was an invitation that pulled in the reader with humor and compelling design and then surprised them by folding out into a poster. The concept was making a funny flowchart that made it impossible for anyone to refuse One Million Degrees' event. That solved the client's invitation requirement. To fulfill the rest, to raise awareness, the folded-out poster was beautiful enough to hang, enabling uninvited others to see it.

64 READY FOR ADVENTURE PRINT | Ad Agency: Peter Mayer Advertising
Creative Directors: Josh Mayer, John Pucci | Art Directors: Tom Futrell
Copywriters: Gary Alipio, Mike Heid | Retouching: Ryan Page | Client: Globalstar

Assignment: Globalstar spent years refining and developing its new satellite technology and products so it could help keep adventurers around the world connected, especially outside of cellular coverage. Innovative as it seems, Globalstar's SPOT came to Peter Mayer to help the company convey compelling story about the brand's adventerous spirit.

Approach: To stress the underlining truth of the Ready for Adventure SPOT brand, we developed a series of ads that highlighted the drama and euphoria of what adventure is all about — the moment of a lifetime. Adventure can go one of two ways, good or bad. The visuals portray this tension and help the adventurers recognize themselves in the ads. The SPOT brand salutes these moments and adventurers — whether they are on or off the grid.

Results: The client was very pleased with the overall design developed to support the launch of its two new products. Globalstar used the creative in both the United States and Canada.

65 LEADVILLE RACE SERIES | Ad Agency: 3e The Life Time Agency
Creative Director: Dustin Schiltz | Client: Life Time - The Healthy Way of Life Company

Credits & Commentary

Assignment: Our goal was to have a flexible design that could be utilized for multiple, nationwide events that captured the renegade spirit of fun and friendship found at off-road mountain biking events created by Life Time and it's brand Leadville Race Series.

Approach: Budget concerns handcuff many great creative ideas. Through our innovative use of digital illustrations and handmade artwork, we can showcase event photography, branding and marketing messaging that can be tailored to the event location, marketing vehicle and timeline.

Results: Pre-race social conversations nearly quadrupled the previous year, registration at all three events and on-site retail sales increased.

67 SIFFCURIOUS | Ad Agency: Wong, Doody, Crandall, Wiener
Executive Creative Director: Tracy Wong | Creative Director: Mark "Monkey" Watson
Art Director: Adam Deer | Copywriter: Peter Trueblood | Art Buyer/Producer: Jessica Obrist
Account Director: Garth Knutson | Account Executive: Anea Klix
Project Manager: Barbara Wilson | Retoucher: Charlie Rakatansky | Studio Artist: Gail Savage
Client: Seattle International Film Festival (SIFF)

Assignment: The Seattle International Film Festival presents more than 400 films from around the globe in just over three weeks. Our task was to generate excitement for the festival among cinephiles, while also making it feel more approachable for a mainstream moviegoing audience. We were tasked with creating a show bill poster, a theatrical trailer, out-of-home executions and a visual tool kit for additional promotional materials.

Approach: The theme of the poster was "Like Moths to a Film." To make the breadth of films more accessible, the festival is broken down into different film genres. So we represented each genre with a different moth. All of the moths were created by local artists, including puppeteers, costume designers and even burlesque performers. And the centerpiece of the poster was a one-of-a-kind, handblown, incandescent light bulb made by Dylan Kehde Roelofs. We shot as much of the poster as we could practically and in camera, including lighting the bulb on a pitch-black set lit with a Tesla coil. We needed to make sure the poster had a special, unique feel because it is also for sale at the festival and is purchased by hundreds of collectors each year. So the bar was high.

Results: Our SIFF clients (who, by the way, are the best clients anyone could ask for) were ecstatic about how well the poster conveyed the energy of the festival and visually tied together various other campaign elements.

68 THE FOLLOWING - COMIC CON POSTER | Ad Agency: FOX Broadcasting Company
Chief Operating Officer, FBC: Joe Earley | Senior Vice President, Design: Thomas Morrissey
Vice President, Design/Print: Mitchell Strausberg | Art Director: Robert Biro
Retoucher: Moises Cisneros | Client: FOX Broadcasting Company

Assignment: To create a poster for the FOX thriller "The Following" to distribute at Comic Con, the yearly convention for entertainment fans.

Approach: "The Following" centers on a former FBI agent, played by Kevin Bacon, who is drawn into a cat-and-mouse pursuit of an erudite, Poe-obsessed serial killer. Because the poster was aimed towards fans of the show rather than a broad audience, we were free to move beyond the conventional star sell or action-oriented entertainment poster. Instead, our imagery reflects the show's underlying dark, gothic themes, incorporating Poe's most famous symbol, the raven.

69 LINCOLN MARATHON STOPWATCH | Ad Agency: Bailey Lauerman
Creative Director: Carter Weitz | Art Director: Marcelo Plioplis
Photographer: Bob Ervin — Ervin Photography | Retoucher: Joe McDermott
Client: Lincoln Marathon

Assignment: The Lincoln Marathon is a long-standing tradition in the city of Lincoln, NE and it has become one of the fastest growing races in the country. This year's concept is tied to the great success of the movie, Lincoln and the tie back to his iconic pocket watch.

Approach: For over 20 years, Bailey Lauerman has had the honor of creating posters and ads for the event. Many runners have been collecting the posters over the years. Our concepts always have to relate to running and include a tie to our beloved president.

Results: Client really loved this iconic approach.

69 SEAGRAPES WINE FESTIVAL | Ad Agency: PP+K
Executive Creative Director: Tom Kenney | Creative Director/Copywriter: Michael Schillig
Art Director: Palmer Holmes | Client: The Florida Aquarium

Assignment: Our assignment was to create a magazine ad for the Florida Aquarium that would promote the Aquarium's annual SeaGrapes Fine Wine and Food Festival. The client wanted us to come up with something that would emphasize the many wines that would be there, while still playing up the unique Aquarium environment where the event was being held.

Approach: We wanted to do something very visual that would promote this wine event in a simple, clever and memorable way. So we designed a fish out of wine corks and then communicated all the splashy details in the copy. Since all of the Aquarium's exhibits would be open during the event, we felt it was important to subtly incorporate a fish in the ad, while still playing up all the wines that would be there.

Results: The ad was very well received by the client. In fact, they liked it so much that they also used this image on a brochure and in other advertising elements for the event. It also seemed to elicit a good response from the public, since attendance at the SeaGrapes Fine Wine and Food Festival was increased from the previous year.

70 ADIDAS Y-3 S/S 2013 | Ad Agency: LLOYD&CO | Creative Director: Doug Lloyd
Art Director: Jason Evans | Client: Adidas

Assignment: Evolve the previous season to create a campaign that encompasses the duality of the Y-3 SS13 pieces.

Approach: With both the print campaign and interactive video, this season explored movement and motion while highlighting the collection's bold colors and graphic lines. The images were stretched and distorted, underlining the visual message.

Results: The client was very pleased with the campaign, as the final images embodied the narrative we set out to relay.

73 OSCAR DE LA RENTA F/W 2012 | Ad Agency: LLOYD&CO | Creative Director: Doug Lloyd
Art Director: Jason Evans | Client: Oscar de la Renta

Assignment: Capture the momentum of the previous season's campaign, while continuing to illustrate the younger, social side of ODLR. The SS13 collection was all about color, so the new campaign needed showcase the details of the collection with an increased focus on accessories.

Approach: For SS13 we set out to create a campaign that was fresh and unexpected. The collaboration between Doug Lloyd, Craig Mcdean and Alex White was one that did just that. A careful edit of the collection, a clean, graphic set design and young fresh casting set the stage for a campaign that delivered strong silhouettes, high-octane color and a modern femininity.

Results: The client was excited with the campaign, as ut received a tremendous response within social media and generated lots of great chatter online.

73 BOTTEGA VENETA S/S 2013 | Ad Agency: LLOYD&CO | Creative Director: Doug Lloyd
Art Director: Conor Hautaniemi | Client: Bottega Veneta

Assignment: To create a campaign that would embody a new chapter of Bottega Veneta's "Art of Collaboration" project.

Approach: We collaborated with photographer Peter Lindbergh and Bottega Veneta's creative director Tomas Maier to capture the cinematic quality of the collection.

Results: The client was very enthusiastic about the final campaign, which ran in all major fashion books.

74 FRM CAMPAIGN | Ad Agency: The Gate | Executive Creative Director: David Bernstein
Associate Creative Director: Mike Abadi, Tim Ryan | Art Director: Tim Ryan
Copywriter: Mike Abadi | Client: GARP

Approach: If the financial crisis taught companies anything, it's that the invisible hand of the marketplace can pack a punch. So you need qualified Financial Risk Managers to limit your risk. The FRM is a globally recognized credential that lets you know if you're hiring someone who has those qualifications. This print campaign visualized the feeling of being hit by the financial crisis in order to highlight the need for more FRMs.

78 GOLD ETF CAMPAIGN | Ad Agency: The Gate
Executive Creative Director: David Bernstein | Associate Creative Director: Mike Abadi,
Tim Ryan | Art Director: Tim Ryan | Copywriters: David Bernstein, Mike Abadi, Tony Gomes
Client: State Street Global Advisors and The Gold Council

Approach: To sell the SPDR Gold Shares ETF, we pointed out that there's nothing quite like gold. To prove the point, we took all the sayings that use the word "gold" and replaced that word with another metal.

81 HOLDING HANDS | Ad Agency: Leo Burnett | Design Director: Alisa Wolfson
Designer: Yoshi Minami | Copywriter: Jake Bogoch | Producer: Richard Blanco | Client: Allstate

Assignment: In 2012, Allstate's "Equality Is" campaign met our objectives and had particularly strong success. A post-campaign survey revealed that the number of LGBT adults in San Francisco and LA who thought Allstate was very committed to the LGBT community increased significantly and Allstate landed in the number one spot among insurance companies with a positive reputation for serving this community. But while Allstate had a strong relationship with the LGBT community in California, on a national level, the brand remained undifferentiated from other insurance companies among LGBT Americans. Given the success and the momentum in California, we wanted to extend our LGBT efforts on a broader scale in 2013, adding in Chicago as an additional market and create a national website that could reach the LGBT community everywhere. The primary goal of the project was to continue building brand affinity amongst an underserved population with significant buying power and brand loyalty. Our message needed to communicate that it's "good to be you." With Allstate and its agents, the LGBT community can always be comfortable being their true self. Allstate knows that showing support for the LGBT community not only makes good business sense, it's simply the right thing to do.

Approach: In an effort to continue building a meaningful connection with the LGBT community, we created a campaign that tapped into a basic truth about this community: While they are just like everyone else in many ways, they still face unique challenges — like being gay in what is still very much a straight world, even with how far we've come. This kind of challenge makes it hard to fully disclose their true selves. Therefore they identify with, appreciate and support others who "get them" and/or are part of the LGBT community themselves. We sought to bring that insight to life through a human lens that only the LGBT community could understand. This landed us on a simple, yet powerful, thought: The simple act of holding your partner's hand is one of the best feelings in the world. It's a gesture that says, "We are connected. We belong together. We are a couple." But for LGBT people, this innocent romantic gesture means publicly outing themselves. And that can be frightening. From there, Out Holding Hands was born — an idea that celebrates the simple, little gesture that binds two people. It stands up for LGBT couples' right to hold hands in public — an act that straight people take for granted. And it's particularly arresting to see two men or two women holding hands in advertising — particularly from a big brand like Allstate. To that end, we decided to make an even stronger statement to the community by running these ads in general market publications like the Red Eye as well as national publications like Out magazine — a small gesture to the straight world, but a huge sign of support to the LGBT community.

Results: The client's reaction was extremely positive, as has been the LGBT community's. Overall, from a digital standpoint, the campaign is performing above established benchmarks. The print ad was picked up by several prominent LGBT and ally blogs, giving greater exposure to the work that was only slated to run in newspaper. A media partnership with BuzzFeed provided significant additional social lift, elevating the visibility of the campaign and increasing affinity for Allstate.

83 "BANKS. US." FOUL POLE AD | Ad Agency: Bailey Lauerman
Creative Director: Ron W. Sack | Copywriter: Nick Main | Art Director: Jim Buhrman
Chief Creative Officer: Carter Weitz | Photographer: Kenny Johnson
Digital Retouch: Gayle Adams, Joe McDermott | Client: CommunityAmerica Credit Union

Assignment: CommunityAmerica Credit Union is a proud sponsor of T-Bones Baseball. The ad concept needed to tout the advantages of having CommunityAmerica as your financial partner while also showing CommunityAmerica's support for T-Bones Baseball.

Approach: Using the "Foul Pole" sign at the stadium allowed us to contrast the differences between banks and CommunityAmerica Credit Union. We positioned the word "Banks" on the "Foul" side and "Us" (CommunityAmerica Credit Union) on the "Fair" side. The copy reads: "Profit payouts, free financial coaching and fewer fees are just some of the ways we always play fair."

Results: Both fans and the client were ecstatic when they saw the ad. One fan who read the ad said, "CommunityAmerica definitely plays fair. They also understand the game of baseball." The ad was also produced as a poster.

84 IMPACT | Ad Agency: QG Propaganda | Creative Director: Marcello Droopy
Art Directors: Mauricio Lo Sardo, Camila Sayuri Miyamura | Copywriters: Daniel Bayer, Tiago Meloni | Print Producer: Alexandre Oliveira | Photographer: Ricardo de Vicq de Cumptich
Marketing Executives: Paulo Eduardo Rossi, Inacio Araujo | Client: MAPFRE Insurance

Assignment: The strategy was to raise awareness amongst drivers of all ages, about the dangers of texting and driving, within a very limited budget for this specific action.

Approach: The agency decided to focus on clients of MAPFRE's associated parking lots, placing parking hangers with strong images of people being struck by cell phones on their rearview mirrors. Although using strong images, they were not aggressive or offensive in any way — on the contrary, they were a beautiful analogy about the dangers of texting and driving.

Results: Since this was a public awareness campaign, it's not possible to quantify how many people stopped texting and driving. Since it's illegal to do it and subject to heavy fines, no one will admit that they used do it in the first place. However, MAPFRE received a large number of compliments from their clients.

89 FOUNDERS BREWING CO. STACKS CAMPAIGN | Ad Agency: DRIVEN
Co-Chief Creative Officers: John Cymbal, Brian Cusac
Client: Founders Brewing Co. Stacks Campaign

Assignment: As Founders AOR, DRIVEN was tasked with developing a market launch campaign for the new Founders beer, All Day IPA. The campaign had two goals: The first was to introduce a brand new session ale that only Founders could make. The second was to position the product in the marketplace as the Founders "go anywhere - do anything" summer beer full of flavor and perfect for folks with an active lifestyle.

Approach: We were delighted when this campaign (agency recommend) was selected to launch All Day IPA. We felt this was the perfect opportunity to produce something unique for the brand. The process was started by researching various locations for the "bottles" to sit upon. Early on we started to gravitate to the comforting feeling of a field museum diorama. In tandem we were reaching out to Photographers that we thought would bring a unique perspective to the project. We received treatments from pure analog to pure digital. We wanted everything to be practical with minimum retouching. In the end we selected Mitch Ranger to shoot the ads and we shot the backgrounds at the Grand Rapids Historical Museum with the base of each "bottle" in their appropriate setting. We then went into the studio and shot the bottle stack ups for three solid days. Each stack shoot started with the base and then the bottle cap, filling in the interior shape of the bottle. Every piece in the stack is practical. All of the C stands, hot glue, broom handles and duct tape were hidden with very minimal removal in post. If you were to see the backside of the bottle it would look like a jumbled scrap pile with no definition at all, but from the camera perspective every curve, angle and bottle cap is loud and clear. After the shoot, it was time for our favorite retoucher to step in and polish the stacks. Jamie Menary worked with us to achieve a sense of realism without pushing a "treatment" for the sake of it. Once again, we wanted to retain the integrity of practical realism that we strived so hard to achieve.

Results: Since introduction of the beer and the campaign, All Day IPA has become the best selling beer in the Founders lineup. Huge consumer demand has created the need for the beer to go from a Founders seasonal offering, to a year round staple.

92 FLAMIN' HOT CHEETOS | Ad Agency: Goodby Silverstein & Partners
Executive Creative Directors: Rick Condos, Hunter Hindman
Associate Creative Directors: Anthony DeCarolis, Erik Fahrenkopf | Art Director: Todd Eisner
Copywriter: Matthew Bottokol | Client: Frito-Lay

Assignment: Cheetos needed a campaign that simply communicated the main point of difference in these Cheetos snacks: they're superhot.

Approach: Our approach: show the aftermath. A half-empty fishbowl covered with Cheetos-dust fingerprints, a fire extinguisher ripped from a wall, a phone with the dust-covered digits suggesting a frantic call to 911 — each of these delivered the "HOT" message while inviting viewers to fill in the narrative blanks.

96 GIVE ME STRENGTH | Ad Agency: Mekanism | Creative Director: Brian Perkins
Art Director: Tom Lyons | Photographer: Blair Bunting | Client: CytoSport

Approach: We designed our Give Me Strength campaign to elevate the Muscle Milk brand and increase awareness with striking simplicity. Its minimalist photography is complimented with direct copy that speaks to a simple truth: strength takes work, and work demands recovery. By showcasing Muscle Milk's stable of elite athlete spokespeople pushing themselves to the limit, we intended to demonstrate that nothing comes easy, even for world-class athletes. It humanizes the idea that no matter who you are, excellence is not an end but a process, and that there is beauty in the struggle.

100 HÄAGEN-DAZS DECONSTRUCTED | Ad Agency: Goodby Silverstein & Partners
Associate Creative Directors: Will Elliott, Patrick Knowlton | Copywriter: Jonathan Pelleg
Art Director: Juan Saucedo | Client: Häagen-Dazs

Assignment: Häagen-Dazs has always talked about the purity of its ingredients. We wanted to highlight the craftsmanship behind their products, showing that Häagen-Dazs is assembled as precisely as other exquisitely crafted masterpieces, such as an Italian stiletto or a concert violin.

Approach: We deconstructed intricately built masterpieces and laid them alongside the ingredients of Häagen-Dazs ice cream to show the world that Häagen-Dazs crafts its ice cream as precisely as Stradiveri crafted a violin.

102 HAIL TO THE CHEESE POSTER SERIES | Ad Agency: RBMM/The Richards Group
Creative Directors: Jeff Barfoot, Chris Smith | Art Director: Jeff Barfoot
Designers: Jeff Barfoot, Brandon DeLoach, Jessica Gavit | Copywriters: Chris Smith,
Wendy Mays, Brittany Sarrett | Client: Central Market

Assignment: Specialty Texas grocer Central Market wanted to promote its annual Cheese Festival, a celebration of over 600 hand-cut, farmstead and artisan cheeses from Texas and around the globe.

Approach: RBMM created the 'Hail to the Cheese' campaign, posing types of cheese as political candidates. The poster series used current (at the time) election year sloganeering and imagery to encourage shoppers to try new styles of cheese.

Results: Sales of cheese and overall sales in the stores during the event were up compared to previous festivals. Posters and other event creatives such as campaign buttons and fake political attack ads trended well on social media outlets and helped increase both store and digital traffic.

104 CHOCOLATE COLLECTION POSTER SERIES |
Ad Agency: RBMM/The Richards Group | Creative Directors: Jeff Barfoot, Chris Smith
Art Director: Jeff Barfoot | Designers: Jeff Barfoot, Jessica Gavit, Kristin Sheehy
Copywriter: Chris Smith | Client: Central Market

Assignment: High-end Texas grocer Central Market wanted to create awareness for its annual Chocolate Festival, the state's largest collection of chocolates, confections and chocolatiers from around the world.

Approach: To promote the festival, RBMM created 'The Chocolate Collection,' a series of posters imitating famous modern artists in order to showcase the event's huge array of products, cooking classes by chocolate experts, recipes and tastings. We drew, dripped and painted (sometimes with real chocolate) our own Warhol, Kandinsky, Seurat, Pollock and Mondrian.

Results: The festival was a great success. Central Market completely booked every cooking class, sold more chocolate than at any of its past chocolate festivals and got people thinking about chocolate in new ways. The reproductions of the posters given away at the event were gone within the first three days.

106 SURPRISE! / A CELEBRATION? | Ad Agency: Populicom, Inc.
Creative Director: Norma Jean Colberg | Art Director: Héctor López
Copywriter: Anabelle Barranco | Photographer: Jorge Ramirez
Client: Pillsbury, B. Fernández & Hnos., Inc.

Assignment: Pillsbury wanted to present all its baking products in one ad.

Approach: Bakery Store Cupcakes are in. For these executions we just added the sprinkles to invite people to bake cupcakes at home.

Results: Pillsbury Puerto Rico's performance surpassed the brand's forecast.

108 LOVE LETTERS | Ad Agency: Shine United | Executive Creative Director: Mike Kriefski
Creative Director/Art Director: John Krull | Copywriter: James Breen
Photographer: Ashton Worthington | Typographer: Holly Dickens | Stylist: Nir Adar
Client: Wisconsin Milk Marketing Board

Assignment: Wisconsin is often thought of as America's Dairyland; however, for many people, this association often conjures up images of cheese heads and mass quantities of commodity cheddar. In fact, the state also offers world-class cheeses, known as some of the best artisanal cheese in the world — with flavor complexity, craftsmanship and originality that rival any cheesemaker across the globe. Our assignment was to communicate the deliciousness and quality of Wisconsin Cheese, to help create awareness for the standard of cheesemaking taking place in America's Dairyland. Setting out, it was our goal to elevate the image of Wisconsin Cheese from ordinary to extraordinary through an impactful print campaign.

Approach: Our creative approach to this print campaign centered on our desire to capture the beauty, creativity and deliciousness of Wisconsin Cheese both visually and textually. Cheese is the world's perfect ingredient, enhancing all foods sweet to savory. That thought helped spark our campaign theme, Wisconsin Cheese Makes Good Food Great — meaning, everything tastes better with cheese on it. To capture that sentiment, our idea came to life through a three-part print campaign featuring love letters written from different foods to Wisconsin Cheese. Ham, macaroni and potato express their appreciation in a handwritten letter, in which each thanks Wisconsin Cheese for elevating it from a simple ingredient, to a delectable dish. Beyond the playful copy, the heroic cheese photography gives the ads the sophisticated and artistic look needed to showcase the craftsmanship of Wisconsin Cheese.

Results: Starting in spring of 2013, the print ads were placed in a variety of epicurean and lifestyle publications and consumer reception could not have been any better. Needless to say, our client was equally as impressed and never fails to let us know.

110 RICH & RARE RESERVE: LIVE RICH PRINT | Ad Agency: Peter Mayer Advertising
Creative Director: Tony Norman | Associate Creative Director: Richard Landry
Copywriter: David Dulock | Art Director: Richard Landry | Client: Sazerac Company, Inc.

Assignment: Sazerac Company, Inc. asked Peter Mayer Advertising to help brand a premium blended Canadian whisky, Rich & Rare Reserve. Targeted at the young urban market, Rich & Rare Reserve is a high-quality alternative to more expensive brands and an upgrade option at a more reasonable price. Our target desires luxury and quality and Rich & Rare Reserve delivers that without being unnecessarily flashy.

Approach: The first step in any assignment is studying the target. From there we created mood boards encompassing relevant aspects of the target's life — who they are, what music they listen to, what brands they associate with, what their everyday environment looks like, how they entertain. We also looked at the competition at higher and lower price points. This process helped solidify a visual language for the brand that both the agency and the client could reference. From there, we created a print unit — in this case, a poster — that brought to life Rich & Rare Reserve's no-nonsense approach to quality and luxury. By creating a bold, typographic treatment chiseled from black concrete, we established Rich & Rare Reserve as a statement brand for the consumer.

Results: Rich & Rare Reserve has quickly established itself as one of the hottest premium Canadian Whisky offerings in the U.S. marketplace, with sales well exceeding expectations. The client, Sazerac Company, plans to accelerate its marketing efforts and spend to take advantage of the very healthy early momentum. The client was extremely pleased with the final execution and has approached Peter Mayer Advertising to work on more brands of Sazerac Company, Inc.

111 HOUSE OF ZWACK ADS | Ad Agency: 160over90 | Chief Creative Officer: Darryl Cilli
Executive Creative Director: Jim Walls | Creative Director: Steve Penning
Designer: Justin LaFontaine | Copywriter: Jill Spradley | Client: Diageo-House of Zwack

Assignment: The House of Zwack liqueurs and the people who drink them are as rich and intriguing as the family behind them. The campaign materials we created reflect this relationship by drawing the connection between the Zwack family's authentic stories and the materials we created.

Approach: We first developed a strategy for the brand. The real insight came when we realized that most liquor brands create fiction around their product but that the HoZ has an authentic and compelling story supporting it. With that in mind the creative team came up with the concept 'Real Character' as it embodies both the stories of the HoZ and the way the product tastes. That served as the platform for which all creative was built and ensured that everything we made is reflective of that idea.

Results: Sales of the HoZ are up 400 percent since the campaign launch.

113 OOMPH CAMPAIGN | Ad Agency: Butler, Shine, Stern & Partners
Creative Director: Tom Coates | Art Director: Gabrielle Tigan | Copywriters: Michael Flannery, Kacey Coburn | Client: ZICO Pure Premium Coconut Water

Assignment: Coconut water is a rapidly growing segment, competing against sodas, juices, sport drinks, energy drinks, teas and waters (both enhanced and the good old fashioned kind). While it's familiar to those living in tropical countries, it's a relatively unknown option to the majority of Americans. Starting in 2004, ZICO built its brand at a grass-roots level among a core consumer segment of yoga and triathlete enthusiasts in key markets. Beginning in 2013, ZICO is being distributed by its majority investor, The Coca-Cola Company. To support this new national distribution, it was time for ZICO to take itself beyond its base of athlete consumers and introduce the unknown brand and unfamiliar product to the masses.

Approach: We knew it was important to maintain the equity built among ZICO's original athlete fans, but also broaden its appeal to this new national presence. We knew it was important to go beyond just the functional benefits of coconut water (natural hydration and replenishment through electrolytes), giving them more meaning and an emotional benefit to the brand. Enter ZICO's new brand campaign: "Oomph." Our way of articulating not only the functional benefit of hydrating with ZICO, but also expanding it to encompass the positive energy we all have inside of us. With this new brand idea, ZICO can appeal to both the athletes looking for oomph to get through

marathons and those of us just looking for some help getting through a long Monday afternoon at work. It's both inspiring and playful, in line with the target's own sense of motivation balanced with realism. It also helps ZICO stand apart from its coconut water competitors who rely on the same tropical or athletic imagery that's become expected from the category. We brought the story to life through a pool of short-form online "Moments of Oomph" videos, outdoor advertising, digital partnerships with health and fitness sites, social media, a refreshed ZICO.com, retail programs and field marketing events.

Results: It's still early, but the new brand idea has given ZICO a fresh way to introduce itself to a broader audience of consumers. The online videos collectively have over 1.5 million views and most importantly sales are growing at a rapid pace.

116 PICKERING TOWN CENTRE FARMER'S MARKET | Ad Agency: Elixir
Creative Directors: Kyle McKenna, Mike Del Rizzo | Client: Pickering Town Centre

Assignment: Pickering Town Centre wanted to promote their Farmer's Market. The purpose of the communication was to create awareness of the market to Pickering residents, encouraging people to buy their produce fresh and locally.

Approach: To help create buzz leading up to opening day of the market, a series of teaser ads were run in out-of-home and on-line media. The creative executions feature things typically found on the farm, placed in everyday settings in the home. The "Bring The Farm Home" campaign was a simple, playful way to communicate the core message to buy farm fresh and local.

Results: Opening day attendance was up 13 percent and sales increased 18 percent over the previous year. The client absolutely loved the creative and has received many positive comments from Farmer's Market tenants and customers alike.

118 KEYSTONE LIGHT | Ad Agency: Saatchi & Saatchi, NY
Creative Directors: Justin Ebert, Alex Lea | Art Director: Ron Villacarillo | Designer: Nate Ripp
Copywriter: Ian Falcon | Client: Keystone Light

Assignment: Promote Keystone Light during the 2014 election.

Approach: Simple. Have Keith Stone — official spokesbro of Keystone Light — throw his sweaty, well-worn trucker hat in the ring for El Presidente of the USA. To do this, we created a series of politically inspired posters that touted Keith's platforms and beliefs. These posters were then handed out during rallys where Keith showed up and signed them. And were also made available via his facebook page, which was temporarily turned into his official Party headquarters.

120 OH, THIS DRESS? | Ad Agency: Heat SF | Photographer: Rodger Hostetler
Art Director: Naomi Duckworth | Account Manager: Megan Robershotte
Client: La Crema Winery

Assignment: The goal of the project was to highlight each of La Crema's distinct varietals and introduce their new Pinot Gris.

Approach: We used Heat's concept of wine specific glassware and stark backgrounds to drive the lighting. Each wine glass was lit to highlight it's unique shape as well as the wine's beautifully subtle differences in shade. The goal was to create a mood of sophistication and romance to contrast with the witty copywriting provided by Heat.

Results: The images have been very successful. They have been used in multiple national magazine campaigns, playful online double banners, as well as a semi-sized truck wrap.

121 CORONA PAINT PARTY | Ad Agency: Zulu Alpha Kilo | Chief Creative Officer: Zak Mroueh
Executive Creative Director: Shane Ogilvie | Art Director: Andrea Romanelli
Copywriter: Kaidy Wong | Studio Artist: Brandon Dyson | Agency Producer: Kate Spencer,
Ola Stodulska | Account Team: Kate Torrance, Dic Dickerson | Media Agency: MEC
Media Team: David Stanton, Natalie Melanson | Event Company: The Hive
Event Team: Skye Brain, Lizzie Short, Stephanie Dowhry | Client: Modelo Molson Imports L.P.

Assignment: After moving away from its long-running iconic Beach campaign, Corona Extra launched its new brand positioning of Live Mas Fina earlier in the year. The new creative platform inspired Canadian millenials to step outside their comfort zone and follow their own path. We wanted to create a multi-sensory activation that brought the notion of Live Mas Fina to life and allow all Canadians to experience what it means firsthand.

Approach: With the help of 208 gallons of paint, we turned an ordinary day into something extraordinary. We threw one of the largest paint parties in Canada at Yonge-Dundas Square. Thousands came as blank canvases. All of them left as works of art. An exclusive Beer Garden opened immediately following the Paint Party where participants enjoyed Coronas and live performances from an impressive lineup of Canadian acts.

Results: Over 7,500 fans RSVP'd on Facebook, overwhelmingly surpassing the 800-person Paint Zone capacity. We filmed the entire experience into an edited online video. In June 2013, it became the 4th most viewed advertising video on YouTube in Canada with over 675,000 views.

122 GROW SISTERHOOD | Ad Agency: The CementBloc
Creative Partners: Elizabeth Elfenbein, Stephanie Berman
Creative Director/Digital: Chauncey O'Neill | Associate Creative Director: Andrew Marvel
Vice Presidents: Andrew Marvel, Chauncey O'Neill | Copywriter: Andrew Marvel
Client: The Coore Foundation

Assignment: Our challenge was to help the Girls Right of Way (GROW) — a small, grassroots non-profit organization — communicate the organization's various programs to perspective donors, partners and project participants. The GROW mission is to provide a path for at-risk girls to realize their full potential. When girls are given the right of way to mature in a supportive, caring environment, amazing things can happen. They, in turn, can guide others and grow healthier, more successful communities.

Approach: A series of ads, posters and postcards communicate the essence of each of the organization's programs including peer counseling (GROW SISTERHOOD), youth orchestra programs (GROW RHYTHM) and reading centers (GROW LITERACY). Each concept reflects the grassroots nature of the organization and conveys the transformative potential of the work being done at GROW.

Results: Having professional materials and project calling cards has helped Girls Right of Way to form important new partnerships with organizations like the Red Cross, both within the US and overseas and a significant increase in project participation has been reported.

123 OU MEDICAL CENTER EDMOND PRINT CAMPAIGN | Ad Agency: BVK
Executive Creative Director: Gary Mueller | Creative Director: Mike Holicek
Copywriter: Mike Holicek | Creative Director/Art Director: Michael Vojvodich
Account Executives: Tricia Lewis, Alicia Schindle | Photographer: Nick Collura
Retoucher: Anthony Giacomino | Client: OU Medical Center Edmond

Assignment: This campaign was created to correct the misperception that OU Medical Center Edmond is an unsophisticated community hospital with little in the way of advanced technology or pioneering procedures. We needed to convince the target that the hospital would exceed their expectations and was therefore the best choice for their family's long-term care. The ads also needed to invite readers to learn more about the hospital's surprising breakthroughs online.

Approach: We needed to memorably convey the idea that OU Medical Center Edmond is bigger, smarter and more advanced than people give them credit for. But simply showing healthcare scenarios such as doctors performing procedures would get lost in the sea of category sameness. We felt a more friendly and approachable direction would be more effective, so we created charming and engaging visual situations that quickly expressed our surprising level of advancement and sophistication. It was a serious message delivered simply and playfully.

Results: The client was pleased with the distinctive look of the campaign and the way it leveraged their longstanding reputation for friendliness while highlighting some of their medical advances. The campaign graphics were extended to an out-of-home poster campaign in area shopping malls and early consumer response was very positive.

124 :) FUEL SERIES / LIFE, LIBERTY AND THE PURSUIT OF :)
Ad Agency: The CementBloc | Creative Partner: Elizabeth Elfenbein
Associate Creative Director/Vice President/Copywriter: Steve Walsh | Client: Happy Fuel LLC

Assignment: The Gross National Happiness Quotient has been operating at a deficit for too long now. And as many studies have shown, reduced happiness can lead to reduced healthiness.

Approach: Social media is the dominant form of communication today. What if we could use the mechanics and tactics of social media, not only for socializing and networking, but as a way to spread happiness? This is how Happy Fuel was born. It began as an iPhone app that gives users a mobile place to store, gauge and share the things that fuel their happy, whether it's a song, photo, video, place, sound, or thought. You simply save your Happy Fuel on your iPhone, and share it on Facebook or Twitter. Happy Fuel also includes a web app, which allows you to store and fuel your happy on your own web page. The launch of Happy Fuel also included a colorful multimedia campaign and fun happy-nings all over New York City, utilizing the oldest form of social media — face-to-face socializing.

Results: Initial uptake has been swift. Happy Fuel is spreading happiness all over the social mediasphere. And when you spread happy, you're also spreading healthy.

126 WWII EXHIBIT BUS SHELTERS | Ad Agency: Peter Mayer Advertising
Creative Director: Tony Norman | Associate Creative Director: Richard Landry
Art Director: Jesse Gresham | Copywriters: Maureen Bongiovanni, David Dulock
Client: The National WWII Museum

Assignment: The National WWII Museum in New Orleans wanted to grow awareness and increase visitation amongst visitors to New Orleans and locals. The "Movie Poster" campaign was launched in February 2013 to build awareness of the interactive experiences at the National WWII Museum and establish the Museum as a must-see New Orleans attraction. The campaign coincided with the opening of the new US Freedom Pavilion: The Boeing Center, adding to the Museum's mission of relating the American experience during WWII and what it means to us today.

Approach: To create the materials for The National WWII Museum's new Freedom Pavilion: The Boeing Center, we took inspiration from the visual style of illustrated movie posters. First, we had CGI models made of the B-17 bomber, My Gal Sal and the Balao-class sub, USS Tang, giving us complete control over the positioning of the objects. We then used stock photos and completely transformed the images through retouching to create compelling, visceral images that capture the drama of war and the experience of visiting the National WWII Museum in New Orleans.

Results: Visitation soared after the launch of the campaign, exceeding visitation goals by 13-25 percent each month. The National WWII Museum experienced a 10 percent increase in visitation over the month prior to the launch and enjoyed a record-setting 90 percent increase in visitation the month after that. The Museum also experienced record attendance for the months of March and July following the launch of the campaign.

127 PICASSO & CHICAGO | Ad Agency: Leo Burnett
Chief Creative Officer: Susan Credle | Art Director: Natalia Kowaleczko
Strategy Director: Kevin Richey | Producer: Kate Piccirilli | Designer: Molly McGee
Design Director: Alisa Wolfson | Client: Art Institute of Chicago

Assignment: The city of Chicago always inspired Picasso, even though he never visited here. The Art Institute wanted revisit that connection in a new exhibition: 100 Years of Picasso & Chicago. And we wanted to celebrate it. So we created a design language, informed by Picasso's art: a playful depiction of his name, a palette reminiscent of his work and a bold call-to-action encouraging Chicagoans to "GO PICASSO".

Approach: We introduced it into the city with the same spirit Picasso intended for all his art: that it be among and enjoyed by the people. It added a pop of color in the greyest months and helped the city experience Picasso before they even set foot in the museum.

Results: The people of Chicago celebrated. They visited the exhibit. And they shared. Most important, they rekindled their relationship with Picasso. One that'll last at least another 100 years.

129 TRUMPETER | Ad Agency: STIR, LLC | Executive Creative Director: Bill Kresse
Senior Art Director: Lee Tse | Associate Creative Director: Scott Shalles | Copywriter: Scott
Shalles | Photographer: Jeff Salzer | Retoucher: Gina Ferrise
Client: United Performing Arts Fund (UPAF)

Assignment: The United Performing Arts Fund (UPAF) supports the performing arts by providing funding and awareness. The print campaign was created to inspire people to donate money to UPAF to support the arts and enhance the community.

Approach: The campaign visually demonstrates the vital role donors play with copy and type that's integrated within the performance depiction. The message communicates that donors play an integral part in the performance arts. Without donations, there wouldn't be a performance.

Results: UPAF received a record number of donations and exceeded their goal of raising over $11 million.

130 GENIUS DOGS | Ad Agency: BBDO Proximity Minneapolis | Art Director: Kelly Gothier
Copywriter: Dave Alm | Executive Creative Director: Brian Kroening
Client: Canine College Training Center

Assignment: Promote Canine College to dog owners as the premiere dog training school.

Approach: The challenge was to do something simple and visual that gets attention while delivering the positive results of Canine College dog behavioral training. By taking well-known intelligent icons and merging them with well-known dog breeds, we created a genius OOH campaign.

Results: In the first month of the campaign, registration for classes at Canine College exceeded expectations, resulting in the addition of more instructors and classes.

133 NUPULSE "THE WAIT IS FINALLY OVER" | Ad Agency: Bailey Lauerman
Creative Directors: Carter Weitz, Ron W. Sack | Designer: Brandon Oltman
Copywriter: Cliff Watson | Photographer: Eric Schmidt | Digital Artist: Rhythm & Hues Studios
Retoucher: Charlie Haygood | Associate Interactive Designer: Patrick Bryan
Production Manager: Gayle Adams | Account Executive: Derek Peterson
Senior Project Manager: Jennifer Kros-Dorfmeyer | Client: Cargill

Assignment: This ad launched a new premium protein source to makers of high-end pet food, so that those manufacturers could offer non-animal, non-corn protein to upscale customers. Pulse protein — made of peas, lentils and fava beans — allowed manufacturers to label their products with consumer-friendly descriptions, like "made from sustainable crops" and "sourced and produced in North America."

Approach: We conducted qualitative research with potential customers and industry experts to understand the unique benefits this new protein source offered to pet food manufacturers, then developed the position that this was the protein that offered all of the benefits manufacturers — and their customers — had been waiting for.

Results: Demand exceeded supply within weeks of the ad's launch.

134 TEENYWEENY LOUDSPEAKERS | Ad Agency: Schneider/Waibel
Creative Directors: Barbara Waibel, Uwe Schneider | Art Director: Kersten Knoedel
Photography: Steffen Jahn | Client: d&b audiotechnik GmbH

Assignment: d&b audiotechnik is a well-known manufacturer of excellent professional loudspeaker systems designed for live performances. For the first time they built extremely small loudspeakers. This is the requested message: Very small professional reinforcement systems for live applications.

Approach: The ad campaign visualizes both sonic sound (curves) and live atmosphere (light). Titles with a wink and helical copy texts — like the visualized curves — tell about the teenyweeny size of these new loudspeakers.

Results: The client is running the campaign in more than 180 special interest magazines round the world.

136 DIRTY PLATES | Ad Agency: Publicis Kaplan Thaler | Chief Creative Officer: Rob Feakins
Creative Director: Scott Davis | Copywriter: Jean Rhode
Photographer: Michael Feher | Client: P&G/Cascade

Assignment: The problem with most dishwasher detergents is that they do not remove all of the food residue so you have to wash a second time. Cascade cleans completely the first time. We wanted to communicate this clearly and simply in a visually arresting way.

Approach: We came up with an idea that dramatizes the problem in a way that hasn't been done before. Eating food on a plate that isn't clean is like still eating the meal from yesterday, so why not create a whole plate out of

that leftover dinner or breakfast? We shoot gorgeous food photography but right on top of this "leftover" plate, showing viewers what happens when your dishwasher detergent doesn't get dishes Cascade clean.
Results: The client loved the campaign.

139 CHEESE GRATER | Ad Agency: Howard, Merrell & Partners
Creative Director: Billy Barnes | Art Director: Chris Gupton | Copywriter: Josh Feuerhelm
Retoucher: Chris Bodie | Client: CORDURA Fabric
Assignment: There are a lot of things out there in the world that will rip, tear, shred and wear fabric out. This campaign had fun with that. Its goal was to remind consumers and host brands that Cordura fabric is the fabric you want when you're out there on your next adventure.
Approach: We looked for things out in the world you might encounter while on a climb or hike, things that were naturally abrasive or threatening to fabric. Then, to exaggerate our point, we married those things with objects that shared graphic similarities and were truly meant to shred, wreck or destroy.
Results: The client was thrilled with how the concept came to life and how unique it was to everything else in the pubs in which it ran. Outdoor retailers requested in-store posters of the ad immediately after launch.

140 OMO LIQUID | Ad Agency: Lowe Vietnam | Designers: Chris Catchpole,
Kumkum Fernando | Photographer: Jonathan Knowles | Client: OMO
Assignment: OMO Liquid is a clothes washing detergent. We were asked to demonstrate the cleaning power of the product on fabrics. So we dramatized this by using a light tablecloth and different liquids spilling onto it.
Approach: The idea was to capture the imagination of the viewer by showing the colour being stripped out of the liquid before it even hits. This way, the viewer gets to work out what's happening — it doesn't matter what spills on your fabrics, OMO Liquid can take out any coloured stains, as if they're just pure water.
Results: It's difficult to attribute direct sales to these press executions, but our clients were delighted with such a creative and visually striking campaign. And 2012 was the best year ever for sales of Unilever's OMO in Vietnam.

142 TIDE PODS | Ad Agency: Saatchi & Saatchi, NY | Creative Director: Daniela Vojta
Client: P&G/TIDE
Assignment: The assignment was to bring the bright and colorful world of Tide Pods to life in print.
Approach: To pull it off, we collaborated with Kai & Sunny to create an optical illusion that aims to "pop" off the page.

143 BREAKFASTER | Ad Agency: BRIGHT RED\TBWA | Executive Creative Director: Rob Kerr
Copywriter: TJ Aseltyne | Art Director: Josh Pittman
Photography/Retouching: We Monsters | Client: Nature's Own
Assignment: Print ad to introduce the Oatmeal Toasters product.
Approach: Oatmeal Toasters are filled with nutritious ingredients like raisins, oats and orange. It's a quick way to get a healthy breakfast. Knowing that speed was the focus, we opted to highlight one possible side effect: highway patrol officers may be looming to give you a speeding ticket.

144 DRY SPILLS | Ad Agency: Publicis Kaplan Thaler | Chief Creative Officer: Rob Feakins
Executive Creative Director: David Corr | Art Director: James Rothwell
Creative Directors: Larissa Kirschner, James Rothwell | Copywriter: Larissa Kirschner
Client: P&G/Bounty
Assignment: The project was to cut through the clutter of paper towel clichés, like side-by-side demos and kitchen wipe-ups. Make something you use everyday into something you think twice about.
Approach: We began with thinking about all the "other" things Bounty could pick up outside of the kitchen, from crime scenes to children learning to potty train. How do real people use paper towels? Although it didn't take us to our final execution, it did make us think differently about Bounty. The path we ultimately took was that Bounty gets spills drier than dry. When you use Bounty the spills dry almost as fast you can make them. So how do we show wet to dry in a new, fun way?
Results: The work has garnered a lot of smiles, a lot of happy clients and when it wins in award shows, a lot of drying of tears.

146 WAHL MASSAGER - BEFORE & AFTER | Ad Agency: Hy Connect
Executive Creative Director: Mark Catterson | Creative Director: Joe Ban
Art Director: Jeff Jasinowski | Copywriter: Erin Watson | Client: Wahl Home Products
Assignment: This ad introduced a new product: the only handheld massager with both hot and cold features. The target was women with active lifestyles (like runners) who wanted new options for pain management.
Approach: Anytime you can get the reader to physically interact with a magazine, you'll get better recall and response. So we designed a split top-bottom layout with corresponding colors to invite interaction. The ad was a quick read that this product offered dual benefits in one massager.
Results: A secondary audience was the trade. This ad and the marketing support helped Wahl get additional distribution with key retailers.

147 PRIDE IN OUR QUALITY SHOWS IN EVERY DELIVERY | Ad Agency: S.O. Creative
Creative Director/Art Director: Sherri Oldham | Designer: Kelly Musebeck
Copywriter: Cameron Miller | Photographer: Barry Fantich | Client: FleetPride
Assignment: With competition increasing in the heavy-duty parts distribution industry, FleetPride identified the need to create new advertising that emphasized the value that FleetPride empoyees bring to the sales experience while underscoring the company's vast choice of quality name parts. As such, the opportunity was to draw a direct correlation from the quality of each FleetPride employee with the quality of products offered.
Approach: To closely link the quality of FleetPride employees with the

quality of the brand name parts offered in store, the concept of making the two blend as one unit came together. To that end, the ad plays off the headline of "Pride in our quality shows in every delivery" by superimposing the image of a FleetPride employee over boxes of parts which are about to be delivered to customers.
Results: The new campaign positively impacted both customers and Fleet-Pride employees alike. In terms of response, the effort resulted in 1,826 click-throughs to FleetPride's website and 624 new customer leads. Furthermore, the campaign was noted to have instilled a strong sense of pride in employees, which in turn increased employee responsiveness to customers.

148 WEIRFOULDS AD CAMPAIGN | Ad Agency: Greenfield/Belser LTD
Creative Director: Burkey Belser | Client: WeirFoulds
Assignment: WeirFoulds needed a new advertising campaign that would be fresh and clever but also flexible enough for the firm's marketing team to run with in the future. The goal was to evolve their five-year-old brand and develop a concept and style that could be used to promote the offerings of each of their unique service areas.
Approach: The WeirFoulds brand is grounded in color — four colors that represent the firm's organization of four service areas. Each base color carries a message relevant to the particular service area to which it relates. Our process began by brainstorming ideas and executions that would work with this core brand reality. We tried several ideas but ultimately wound up with the final approach as we felt it beautifully captured the essence of the firm's energy, focus and intelligence.
Results: The client was absolutely thrilled with this new creative. The anecdotal feedback they've received has also been enthusiastic and overwhelmingly positive. The team has done an excellent job leveraging this new creative to evolve their brand across all their marketing channels.

151 TOP OF THE ROCK, DECK THE HOLIDAY SERIES | Ad Agency: Pentagram Design
Art Director: Michael Gericke | Designers: Michael Gericke, Matt McInerney, Kelly Sung
Client: Tishman Speyer
Assignment: Create a bold and fun new holiday campaign for Top of the Rock — New York's most iconic place for the holidays.
Approach: To capture the holiday spirit of New York, Pentagram created a campaign that featured the tagline "Deck the Holidays," a play on "deck the halls," and bright graphics that combined holiday symbols like snowmen, reindeer and Christmas trees with the familiar forms of the deck's viewfinders and the iconic architecture of the Center.
Results: The campaign was a success.

153 ROCKAFELLER CENTER, THE PLAZA CAFE | Ad Agency: Pentagram Design
Art Director: Michael Gericke | Designers: Michael Gericke, Matt McInerney, Kelly Sung
Client: Tishman Speyer

155 THE REAL BEASTS | Ad Agency: PP+K | Executive Creative Director: Tom Kenney
Creative Director: Michael Schillig | Copywriter: Michael Schillig
Art Director: Palmer Holmes | Client: Big Cat Rescue
Assignment: Big cats that are raised as pets and exploited for profits often end up being abused, abandoned and even killed. Our assignment was to create a poster for the Big Cat Rescue Sanctuary that would capture people's attention and convey that those individuals who try to domesticate wild animals are the real beasts. Ultimately, our objective was to get people to call or email their elected local representative and urge them to support the Big Cats & Public Safety Protection Act. If enacted, this law would protect big cats by prohibiting the private possession, exploitation and breeding of these wild animals.
Approach: We set out to design a poster that would pull viewers in through the sheer power of the visual. So we applied a tiger's snarling mouth to a human face in order to portray people who try to domesticate wild animals as the most ruthless beasts of all. We knew this visual had to emotionally touch people and inspire them to take action by calling or emailing their elected local representative and encouraging them to support the Big Cats & Public Safety Protection Act.
Results: This poster was well received by Big Cat Rescue. It has elicited quite a response from the many individuals who have seen it while taking a tour of the 55-acre Big Cat Rescue Sanctuary, which is home to over 100 abandoned, abused and orphaned exotic cats. It has led to many calls and emails to local elected representatives. Most importantly, such strong support has helped keep the Big Cats & Public Safety Protection Act alive as an important bill in the House and Senate that could one day become a law to protect big cats from being kept as pets or held in miserable roadside zoos.

156 YOU ARE FINE / BABY YOU'RE THE ONE BUS SHELTERS | Ad Agency: Serve
Creative Director: Gary Mueller | Copywriter: Nick Pipitone | Art Director: Michael Vojvodich
Client: United Way of Greater Milwaukee
Assignment: The campaign is part of a long running teen pregnancy prevention marketing effort in Milwaukee. The goal of the campaign is to deglamorize teen pregnancy, by showing teens — in this case girls — the reality of how hard it is to raise a baby and that they'll likely raise it alone.
Approach: We wanted to create an outdoor campaign that was unique and that spoke to kids where we knew they had time on their hands to consume the same message every single day. So we created a bus shelter campaign targeting high school students outside of high schools with the highest teen birth rates. To get girls attention, we used the same seductive, smooth-talking approach that guys use to get girls into bed. By showing good look-

ing young men looking longingly into the camera (as if they were looking at their girlfriend), each ad uses a conventional opening "pick up" line; i.e. "Baby, you're the one." The long copy then pivots to the reality that if their girlfriend gets pregnant, chances are their guy isn't sticking around and they're going to be stuck raising their child.

Results: This campaign is part of a series of marketing campaigns that have shown a 35 percent drop in teen pregnancy rates over the past five years. The campaign was recently honored by the White House's Committee for Community Solutions.

159 OVER QUALIFIED INTERNS | Ad Agency: Zulu Alpha Kilo | Creative Director: Zak Mroueh
Art Director: Bhavik Gajjar | Copywriter: Nick Asik | Photographer: Rob Fiocca
Digital Imaging: Mo Elabi, Nabil Elsaadi | Mac Artist: Jamie Morren, Keeley O'hara, Mo Elabi
Agency Producer: Kari Macknight Dearborn | Account Director: Sherryl Woodward
Client: National Advertising Benevolent Society (NABS)

Assignment: The National Advertising Benevolent Society (NABS) Vintage Intern Auction is a Canadian ad industry charity event where the country's top ad execs are auctioned off as interns for the day. The brief was to raise awareness of the auction and ultimately to generate donations via bids. The target was Canada's advertising and marketing community.

Approach: To promote the auction, we created a series of posters featuring cheekily written letters from top ad execs such as Sid Lee's Philippe Meunier and Dove Evolution Creative Director Nancy Vonk, asking for an internship. The items surrounding each letter hold significance to the vintage intern's career and image. Posters were placed in the washrooms of advertising and marketing companies across Canada.

Results: The NABS Vintage Intern Auction exceeded its fundraising goals by 25 percent. The campaign generated buzz throughout the Canadian advertising industry, appearing on all the top Canadian advertising news outlets and blogs.

162 SPAY/NEUTER | Ad Agency: Meers | Creative Director: David Thornhill
Art Director: Brandon Bennett | Designer: Taylor Pruitt | Photographer: Ron Berg
Retoucher: Tiffany Matson | Client: Great Plains SPCA

Assignment: Spay/Neuter is one of those veterinary services that is strange to talk about. And while the topic itself is strange, the result of the service on animals is extremely beneficial to all pets and unwanted animals. You have the procedure done for the greater good of the community. Cats and dogs "will play" so to speak. The goal of this campaign was to raise awareness of the spay/neuter service.

Approach: It seemed appropriate to take this strange conversation head on and simply add a little humanity, in the form of slang. The decision was made to feature a very simple, beautiful image of a dog/cat and to contrast this image with provocative typography that suggests the human understanding of "cating around" if you will. It's difficult to think of a cute fluffy cat as a floozy.

Results: Top of mind awareness of Great Plains SPCA grew 14 percent over a 6-month period with an 11 percent aided recall on this specific campaign. Spay/Neuter services continue to increase as the overall health of animals improves in the Kansas City metro area.

165 RECIPEACE | Ad Agency: Leo Burnett | Global Chief Creative Officer: Mark Tutssel
Chief Creative Officer: Susan Credle | Executive Creative Director: Jeanie Caggiano
Creative Director: Matt Miller, Phil Jungmann | Design Director: Alisa Wolfson
Copywriter: Adam Ferguson | Art Director: Kate Harding-Jackson
Senior Designer: Kelly Dorsey | Photographer: Chriss Cassidy
Executive Director of Production: Vincent Geraghty | Group Executive Producer: Rob Tripas
Senior Producer: Laurie Gustafson | Client: Peace One Day/D&AD

Assignment: In 2001, Peace One Day worked with the UN to create Peace Day, a global day of nonviolence meant to create peace in the lives of the individual and the community. But low awareness and participation have prevented Peace Day from reaching its potential. Peace One Day challenged us to create a scalable campaign that helps raise awareness and participation in Peace Day.

Approach: The Recipeace campaign focused on two things. First, we wanted to clearly communicate the idea of peace in a new way. In our campaign, we used common war weapons juxtaposed with food to show how the simple act of breaking bread can resolve conflict. We then created a pastel palette, elegant typography and quiet messaging to illustrate our peaceful objective. We also created silk-screened olive oil bottles that served as the campaign's centerpiece. Placed on restaurant tables throughout Chicago, they inspired diners to break bread together as a first gesture toward settling their differences on Peace Day.

Results: Recipeace launched in Chicago and in under four weeks, was embraced by hundreds of restaurants, grocers, chefs and foodies, who each used the campaign elements to spread the word to the general public. From there, the campaign grew through websites, publications and people around the world. Ultimately, Recipeace generated over 2.3 million earned media impressions, thousands of tweets worldwide and countless peace dinners throughout Chicago. More importantly, millions were made aware of Peace One Day's mission and the global community came closer to achieving peace, one meal at a time.

168 ADOPT A DOG | Ad Agency: Meers | Creative Director: David Thornhill
Art Director: Brandon Bennett | Photographer: Ron Berg
Retoucher: Tiffany Matson | Client: Great Plains SPCA

Assignment: Pet adoption is often an emotional experience. New pet owners

are typically attracted to pets for reasons very personal and cannot often say why. They simply had to have it. Meers discovered that most pet owners either prefer dogs or cats, but seldom both. Some people are just dog people, others are just cat people. It's just the way it is. The creative idea was to simply use one pet to get to the other, and in so, create a newfound admiration for a type of pet. The objective was to get more pets adopted by getting a pet friendly audience to consider pets they haven't yet considered.

Approach: We peeled back a lot of different layers on what it means to adopt a pet. The emotional satisfaction, the idea of creating a new friend. It all started to sound the same. We knew that to differentiate, we would have to come at this completely backwards. So we did. The solve was to make dog advocates into cat advocates. And vise versa. Which in turn, would get more animals adopted.

Results: Top of mind awareness of Great Plains SPCA grew 14 percent over a 6-month period with a 27 percent aided recall on this specific ad. Adoptions continue to increase with an average of 32 a day. Another measure of a successful advertising campaign is a happy Executive Board.

169 NO PLACE FOR A KING | Ad Agency: PP+K | Executive Creative Director: Tom Kenney
Creative Director: Michael Schillig | Copywriter: Michael Schillig
Art Director: Palmer Holmes | Client: Big Cat Rescue

Assignment: Big cats that are raised as pets and exploited for profits often end up outgrowing their owners and face horrific living conditions, abuse and even abandonment. Our assignment was to create a poster which would convey the lack of space, food and brutality these animals are often subjected to by private, profit-hungry owners. Ultimately, we wanted to inspire people to call or email their elected local representative and urge them to support the Big Cats and Public Safety Protection Act. If enacted, this law would protect big cats by prohibiting the private possession, exploitation and breeding of these wild animals.

Approach: We set out to design a poster that would communicate the appalling conditions, hunger and pain these majestic big cats often faced, when raised as pets or exploited for profits at miserable roadside zoos. We knew this visual had to catch people's attention and inspire them to take action by calling or emailing their elected local representative and encouraging them to support the Big Cats and Public Safety Protection Act.

Results: This poster has touched many people's hearts and led them to call or email their local elected representatives. Most importantly, such strong, unified support has helped to keep the Big Cats and Public Safety Protection Act alive as an important bill in the House and Senate that could one day become a law to protect big cats from being kept as pets or held in miserable roadside zoos.

**170 "TEEN LIFE WON'T CHANGE - CHEERLEADER" POSTER /
BASKETBALL" POSTER** | Ad Agency: Serve | Art Director: Casey Christian
Copywriter: Stephanie Goldner | Creative Director: Gary Mueller
Account Executive: Matt Larson | Photographer: Jeff Salzer | Retoucher: Anthony Giacomino
Client: United Way of Greater Milwaukee

Assignment: The goal of the campaign was to change teen's perceptions about the difficulties of teen pregnancy. And show them that adding a baby into their life will make it much harder for them to do the kinds of things they enjoy doing now.

Approach: So we created a campaign that was visually awkward and caught attention from area teenagers. The visual of an athlete performing an extremely physical action with a baby strapped to a chest is paired with a short, effective message; "Think your teen life won't change with a baby?" This compelling, unexpected message forces teenagers to think about the immediate consequences having a baby as a teenager will have in their lives and the hobbies they will have to give up. This harsh insight, combined with a surprising visual is an excellent way to communicate our message.

Results: Teen pregnancy dropped 10 percent in the past year and 35 percent over the past 5 years. The campaign was recently honored by the White House's Committee for Community Solutions.

172 AIGA DESIGN FOR GOOD POSTER CAMPAIGN — AMERICAN RED CROSS
Ad Agency: Lewis Communications | Art Director/Associate Creative Director: Roy Burns
Designer: Roy Burns | Copywriter: Kathy Oldham | Client: AIGA

Assignment: Design for Good, an initiative of AIGA (American Institute of Graphic Arts), is a national platform to build and sustain the implementation of design thinking for social change. In the fall of 2012 (and in honor of its 25th anniversary), the Birmingham area chapter of AIGA held a fundraising poster competition on the theme of Design for Good, judged by internationally renowned poster artist Luba Lukova. Our entry was a two-poster campaign, created for the American Red Cross, designed to encourage blood donations during the crisis of last year's national blood shortage.

Approach: The posters aim to project a simple, yet powerful evocation of need for donors.

174 HOLIDAY HORROR | Ad Agency: Zulu Alpha Kilo | Creative Director: Zak Mroueh
Copywriter: Nick Asik | Art Director: Mooren Bofill | Photographer: Vicky Lam
Photography Studio: Westside Studio | Photographer's Assistant: Alex Beetham
Model Maker/Stylist: Jamie Oxenham, Oxenham Design | Client: Fangoria Entertainment

Assignment: Fangoria is the world's number one horror magazine. The assignment was to promote magazine subscriptions around the holiday season — not a season typically associated with horror.

Approach: We combined visuals representative of 'horror' with everyone's favourite holiday cookie — the gingerbread man. We created a series of posters featuring gingerbread men doing horrible things to one another.

Results: The posters launched in December 2012. They received a lot of buzz online, being featured on numerous blogs, websites and throughout social media. Further, the posters succeeded in increasing magazine sales into 2013.

177 NIV SUNRISE | Ad Agency: Extra Credit Projects | Creative Director: Rob Jackson
Art Director: Aaron Sullivan | Designer: Alissa Klee, Allison Supron | Photographer: Andy Terzes
Client: Zondervan Publishers

Assignment: This two-page spread ad aimed to promote the NIV translation.

Approach: Inspired by morning light, we used the imagery of a sunrise as a metaphor for the light that is shed on Bible readers across the world as they pick up the NIV Bible, which is easier to read and understand than other Bible translations. Ultimately, we wanted to keep the ad simple and engaging.

Results: The client was thrilled with the final product and it quickly went to print in a number of Christian publications.

178 BOGUE'S DINER CAMPAIGN | Ad Agency: Lewis Communications
Creative Director: Spencer Till | Photographer: Jeff Williams | Copywriter: Stephen Curry
Client: Bogue's Diner

Assignment: Bogue's Diner is a cherished local institution in Birmingham, Alabama. It's unpretentious, the food is comforting and familiar, and the same cast of characters has been behind the counter and in the seats for generations. In a city that was rapidly filling with national chains, our mission was to differentiate the restaurant and remind consumers that they had a more authentic alternative.

Approach: Our campaign simply sought to shine a spotlight on that authenticity, and remind people of the incredible devotion patrons feel for this place. In a world where a chain restaurant on every corner is rapidly becoming the norm, it's reassuring to know that there's a place where warmth and authenticity continue to rule the day.

182 JESUS FISH | Ad Agency: DeVito/Verdi | Creative Director: Sal DeVito
Art Director: Manny Santos | Copywriter: Barry Flanik | Agency Producer: John Doepp
Photographer: Robert Ammirati | Client: Legal Sea Foods

Assignment: Legal Sea Foods is always looking to stretch their advertising dollar and thus charges us every year to find effective advertising concepts that really break through the clutter.

Approach: Taking advantage of the cultural phenomenon surrounding the Christian "Fish" symbol that often appears on the backs of cars, along with the many other popular "Fish" symbols derived from it (see this site for the plethora of "Fish" available: http://evolvefish.com/fish/emblems.html), we decided who better to have their own "Fish" than Legal Sea Foods. Aimed at adults living in the Boston area, The Fish has run in magazine print and on taxi tops in Boston, where Legal Sea Foods is an established icon in itself, with the simple line "It's a religious experience" locked up with the Legal Sea Foods logo. The stark white background and simplicity of the concept definitely helped it stand out amongst street traffic (taxi tops) and other magazine ads.

Results: The client was extremely impressed with this ad, which generated a lot of buzz and talk value in the marketplace.

183 REALLY GOOD BURGER | Ad Agency: PP+K | Executive Creative Director: Tom Kenney
Creative Director: Michael Schillig | Copywriter: Michael Schillig | Art Director: Palmer Holmes
Client: Big Boy Restaurants International, LLC

Assignment: Our assignment was to create an in-store poster that would clearly communicate the details of a charitable promotion that was being held during the grand opening of a Big Boy® restaurant. We wanted to emphasize in a strong way that a portion of the proceeds from the purchase of a Double Deck Cheeseburger would benefit the Friendship Centers of Emmet County Meals On Wheels program.

Approach: When you say that a burger is "good," most people think you mean good tasting. So we wanted to come up with a simple but powerful way to convey that this burger was a lot more than just good tasting. By ordering the Double Deck Cheeseburger, people would be doing a really good deed for those in need. So we showcased just how good the burger was by placing a little halo over it and then communicated how proceeds from it would go to the Friendship Centers of Emmet County Meals On Wheels program.

Results: The poster was positively received by the client and consumers at the grand opening of this Big Boy® restaurant. It really got their attention and contributed to increased sales for the Double Deck Cheeseburger during the grand opening week of this promotion. So both Big Boy and the Friendship Centers of Emmet County Meals On Wheels program came out as big winners. And everyone was literally left with a good feeling inside.

184 ARIEL PLATES | Ad Agency: Beacon/Leo Burnett, Tokyo
Executive Creative Director: Jon King | Creative Directors: Keizo Mugita, Shuji Matsumura
Art Director: Norihiro Sasa | Copywriter: Minoru Hongo | Designers: Chizuru Horikawa,
Yuichiro Yoshino | Agency Producers: Kozo Nagashima, Makiko Okada
Photographer: Fumio Doi | Photo Retoucher/Director: Sunao Sakurai | Stylist: Masato Okamura
Print Run: Toshifumi Narui | Client: P&G Ariel

Assignment: Quickly and impactfully show Japanese housewives that the unique new benefit of Ariel Revo's Stain Resistant laundry detergent can make clothes easier to wash the next time.

Approach: We took the one thing that is both easy to wash when it's dirty and has a connection to food (a primary cause of stains)…the plate. By making real plates in the shape of clothes with problematic food we sug-

gested that no matter how you dine you no longer have to fear ruining your clothes. Ariel protective pre-wash makes laundry easy.

Results: This graphically pleasing series of ads was well-liked by Japanese housewives and women. Achieved Dentsu Advertising Awards Best in Category, selected to Japan APA Awards, EPICA Book 26 and Lurzer's Archive.

186 THE FUTURE IS BRIGHT | Ad Agency: Peter Mayer Advertising
Creative Director: Eddie Snyder | Art Director: Nathan McCollum | Copywriter: Jason Otis
Client: Peter Mayer Advertising

Assignment: Per our longtime agency traditions, we create a poster annually that we mail to our contacts — clients, prospects, vendors, friends — commemorating the 4th of July. Sometimes sober and reverent, sometimes whimsical and gently fun, our posters involve a team effort with creative types, interns, and any employee from any department who wants to play, coming together to design an Independence Day poster that reflects our cultural brand while honoring our nation.

Approach: Americans have had a few difficult years lately. There's been war, economic hardship and political strife. Our objective in this piece was to strike a hopeful, inspiring note. We did it by presenting perhaps the most iconic of American symbols — the Statue of Liberty — with a slight twist, illustrating our message: that there are good times ahead, our future is bright.

187 WEAPON | Ad Agency: PP+K | Executive Creative Director: Tom Kenney
Creative Director: Michael Schillig | Copywriter: Nick McMurdy
Art Director: Trushar Patel | Client: PP+K

Assignment: Our agency, PP+K, has a long-standing relationship with the Pediatric Cancer Foundation, which is an organization dedicated to eradicating childhood cancer. We had the opportunity to create a poster for a fishing tournament that raises money and awareness for the PCF's mission.

Approach: Cancer doesn't fight fair. So we figured, we need to find other ways to fight back. Visually, we started with an object germane to a fishing tournament — a fishing pole. We noticed that it resembled the scope of a gun. We then used bold, thought-provoking copy to fill in the rest of the "gun" image and give context to the visual. The single-minded message that the viewer takes away is that we aren't just fishing — we're joining a serious fight.

Results: Since the client was technically our own agency, we created a piece that our company can be proud of, from both a creative and philanthropic standpoint. Our concept resonates with anyone who dedicates their time and money to fighting this horrible disease. At the end of the day, it's a memorable execution that further displays our support for the PCF and continues PP+K's commitment to the cause.

188 AMERICA'S CUP 2013 | Ad Agency: Michael Schwab Studio | Designer: Michael Schwab
Client: James Whitburn, America's Cup 2013

Assignment: Michael Schwab Studio was commissioned to commemorate the 2013 America's Cup sailing event hosted by San Francisco's Golden Gate Yacht Club.

Approach: I wanted to create a graphic image that evoked the beauty, power and drama of this historic event. My strategy was to avoid technical nautical design details and run with a 'less is more' approach, typical of my style.

Results: The client was very happy with the results. I received several positive and intriguing comments such as 'Looks like sharks in the water'. 'The tilted water/horizon line really feels like the viewer is in motion'. 'The Golden Gate Bridge is a mythical presence watching over the race'.

189 NATIONAL ENDURANCE BAREFOOT CHAMPIONSHIPS POSTERS
Ad Agency: BVK | Creative Director: Gary Mueller | Copywriters: Nick Pipitone, John Krill
Art Director: Michael Vojvodich | Photographer: Nick Collura | Client: Footstock

Assignment: Promote Footstock, the National Endurance Barefoot Water Ski Championships. But more importantly, outdo 20 years of amazing poster concepts, that have not only created a cult-like following for the event around the country, but for a loyal group of collectors of the annual poster.

Approach: Because most of the winners do have extraordinarily large feet, we decided to focus on the unfair advantages that some competitors are seemingly born with. Of course, everyone knows that in advertising you can never lose by showing babies and in barefooting, everyone loves crazy large feet. So the concept of having cute babies with giant feet seemed perfect.

Results: The event saw a 13 percent increase in the skiers and a 22 percent increase in attendance. What's more, the posters instantly became some of the most popular in tournament history. After announcing at the event that the remaining posters were available for free, 300 posters were given out in less than 10 minutes. The posters were also the feature of an article in Water Ski Magazine.

191 SUPER NATURAL | Ad Agency: Bold Worldwide
Creative Director/Art Director: Ahab Nimry | Executive Creative Director: Brian Cristiano
Copywriter: Jake Edinger | Photographer: Brian Kuhlmann | Client: Weider Nutrition

Assignment: I was contacted to create dynamic images for an all-natural nutritional supplement for Crossfit athletes. The images would be appearing in national fitness magazines and needed to stand out to the reader among all the other supplement advertising.

Approach: We came up with the idea of superheroes taking the supplement. We liked the play on words with super hero and nutrition, thus creating the super natural. We choose camera angles that could be easily rotated, creating the feel of super heroes doing super feats in the resulting image.

Results: These images are compelling and attention-grabbing. We don't have any sales results but all feedback has been very "strong."

194 HONOR THE GAME POSTERS | Ad Agency: Peter Mayer Advertising
Creative Director: John Pucci, Josh Mayer | Art Director: Jesse Gresham
Associate Creative Director: Mike Heid, Tom Futrell | Retouching: Dan Tierney, Ryan Page
Client: Marucci Sports

Assignment: For years, Marucci had built its reputation as a premium bat maker by word of mouth among major baseball league baseball players. While the quality of its products spoke for themselves, Marucci's outward communication didn't reflect the company's respect for the game. So Marucci turned to Peter Mayer to build a new brand that captured its commitment to baseball. One of the first opportunities to display Marucci's new brand was a premium insert in Baseball America, the country's foremost publication for those who are students of the game. This piece would be Marucci's flag in the ground — a declaration of what Marucci is all about to the nation's elite baseball players.

Approach: Rather than using this prime real estate for a product-driven ad, we decided to create a piece that would allow the new brand to live beyond the pages of Baseball America. To bring the emotion and authenticity of "Honor the Game" to life, we created a two-sided poster that allowed dedicated athletes to choose how they express their commitment to the game. On the one side we featured Albert Pujols in a way that reflected the collective spirit of Albert, the Marucci brand and the dedicated athletes that read Baseball America. On the other hand it is a tip of the cap to those that get up every morning to improve their game.

Results: The client was incredibly pleased with how this piece gave their brand a distinct voice it never had before. They were so happy with the piece that they reprinted it and gave away posters at the American Baseball Coaches Association Convention.

196 DANCER | Ad Agency: STIR, LLC | Executive Creative Director: Bill Kresse
Senior Art Director: Lee Tse | Associate Creative Director: Scott Shalles
Copywriter: Scott Shalles | Photographer: Jeff Salzer | Retoucher: Gina Ferrise
Client: United Performing Arts Fund (UPAF)

Assignment: The United Performing Arts Fund (UPAF) supports the performing arts by providing funding and awareness. The print campaign was created to inspire people to donate money to UPAF to support the arts and enhance the community.

Approach: The campaign visually demonstrates the vital role donors play with copy and type that's integrated within the performance depiction. The message communicates that donors play an integral part in the performance arts. Without donations, there wouldn't be a performance.

Results: UPAF received a record number of donations and exceeded their goal of raising over $11 million.

197 BEHOLD — SHAKARA LEDARD | Ad Agency: BRIGHT RED\TBWA
Executive Creative Director: Rob Kerr | Associate Creative Director: Jason Piroth
Photographer: Robb Aaron Gordon | Retoucher: Patrick White
Client: The Islands Of The Bahamas

Assignment: Part of our ongoing campaign to showcase the beauty and diversity of the many islands that make up The Bahamas.

Approach: Inagua is home to a colony of 20,000 endangered flamingos. This ad paired these beautiful birds with another rare Bahamian beauty: supermodel, Shakara Ledard.

Results: Visitors to The Islands Of The Bahamas increased significantly after the launch of the campaign.

197 BEHOLD — DAVID COPPERFIELD | Ad Agency: BRIGHT RED\TBWA
Executive Creative Director: Rob Kerr | Associate Creative Director: Jason Piroth
Photographer: Robb Aaron Gordon | Retoucher: Patrick White
Client: The Islands Of The Bahamas

Assignment: Part of our ongoing campaign to showcase the beauty and diversity of the many islands that make up The Bahamas.

Approach: Not only is David Copperfield one of the most famous illusionists of all time, he is also the owner of a spectacular resort in The Exumas. This ad focused on the breathtaking beauty of this very special place.

Results: Visitors to The Islands Of The Bahamas increased significantly after the launch of the campaign.

199 TOP OF THE ROCK, ANY POINT OF VIEW SERIES
Ad Agency: Pentagram Design | Art Director: Michael Gericke | Designers: Michael Gericke, Matt McInerney, Kelly Sung | Client: Tishman Speyer

201 2012 FIESTA HEN | Ad Agency: Proof Advertising | Creative Directors: Craig Mikes, George Ellis | Art Director: Drew Hammond | Copywriter: Randall Kenworthy
Client: San Antonio Tourism

Assignment: Fiesta San Antonio is an 11-day party with events that celebrate San Antonio's unique heritage. With over 100 official family-friendly events including parades, coronations, art exhibits, food and more, there is plenty to choose from to create your own Fiesta experience. While Fiesta has been held since 1891, its exposure hadn't grown much outside the San Antonio area.

Approach: Our approach was to create a symbol for the event that was unique and memorable. Mardi Gras has beads. Fiesta has cascarones (brightly colored, hollowed eggs filled with confetti) and now the multi-colored hen that presumably laid them.

Results: Increased interest in Fiesta reflected by a +149 percent traffic to our Fiesta landing page on visitsanantonio.com. Increased intent to travel to San Antonio for Fiesta reflected by a +38 percent views of Fiesta hotel packages on visitsanantonio.com. Fans of the ad requested reprints forcing us to reprint as posters for giveaways.

202 POOL | Ad Agency: New Moment New Ideas Company Y&R | Designers: Svetlana Copic, Slavisa Savic, Nemanja Spoljaric | Client: Kielo Travel Agency

Assignment: The goal was to promote easy and convenient, custom made services of the travel agency to overworked, overstressed professionals.

Approach: We wanted to capture the moment when one is feeling stuck and overwhelmed at work, fantasizing about getting out of the office and taking a holiday. The idea originated from the fact that when our minds wander, we doodle, and doodles offer a true, uncensored window into our thoughts, feelings and desires at a given moment. The ad is supposed to inspire one to really do something this time, to act according to the dream.

Results: The feedback we received was that the TG had a strong sense of recognition and was able to fully identify with the ad. Simplicity of the execution made the ad universally understandable and made it feel unpretentious and honest.

204 TRAVEL GOLF / FISHING | Ad Agency: The Richards Group
Creative Directors: Jimmy Bonner, Rob Baker | Art Director: Jimmy Bonner
Copywriter: Rob Baker | Photographer: Andy Anderson | Client: Sea Island

Assignment: Differentiate Sea Island from other high-end resorts and attract new guests by capturing the gracious hospitality enjoyed by generations of families who crossed that bridge and formed a special bond with the island.

Approach: This campaign is all about welcoming guests with open arms. It's about raising the energy of Sea Island by exploring all the things there are to do once you cross the bridge. And it's about tapping into the very nature of human beings when they discover something special: Do you share it? Or do you keep it entirely to yourself?

Results: Following the launch of the campaign and on a very modest budget, bookings were up for five of the six months that are most crucial to their season.

205 GLYDE OUTDOOR CAMPAIGN | Ad Agency: Hub Strategy
Creative Directors: DJ O'Neil, Peter Judd | Associate Creative Director: Jason Rothman
Designer: Jason Rothman | Illustrator: Jason Rothman | Copywriter: Leona Frey | Client: Glyde

Assignment: Glyde allows you to sell your old iPhone online for more money than you would get elsewhere, which is great, except people didn't know Glyde existed. They asked us to create an out-of-home campaign in San Francisco to get the word out.

Approach: We wanted to do something different than we were used to seeing around town. Something that would be fun and pop on the crowded streets and public transportation in San Francisco. Rather than resorting to the usual slick product photography, we created a cast of illustrated characters targeting users in the tech industry who are likely to have old gadgets lying around. The message in their talk bubbles was simple: Don't be an idiot. Sell your old iPhone and make $300.

Results: After running the campaign for only four weeks, the number of old iPhones listed on Glyde almost tripled and the tech geeks proved (as if we didn't already know) that they were definitely not idiots.

207 NAVARRO SAXOPHONE MOUTHPIECES | Ad Agency: Mangos
Creative Director: Bradley Gast | Art Directors: Jane Gast, Bradley Gast
Copywriters: Bradley Gast, Joanne de Menna | Photographer: Michael Furman
Web Programmer: John McCartney | Client: Navarro Saxophone Mouthpieces

Assignment: The mouthpiece is the most personal part of the saxophone. Rafael Navarro, a mouthpiece artist, crafts museum-like pieces that straddle the line between tradition and innovation. As he launched an online-only company to sell these spectacular pieces, the challenge was to create a site that performed as beautifully as the product itself. An e-commerce experience that was flawlessly simple, and rich media that would generate buzz.

Approach: Since Navarro mouthpieces are only available online, the presentation of the product, as well as the user experience, was absolutely critical — even more so with prices that range from $575 to $750. We needed to package all of the content that a serious musician would need to make an informed decision, without compromising the elegant openness of the site's design. The endorsements from some of the best players in the world brought instant and powerful credibility to the quality of Navarro mouthpieces. Players like Wayne Shorter and Bob Mintzer are legends. We used video shot during personal fitting sessions with these players and packaged the content into two-minute movies. With no ad budget, social media was the perfect way to spread the word about the new premium line of Navarro mouthpieces. Threads on online forums like SaxOnTheWeb generated talk weeks before the website launched. Now that the site is live, YouTube, Twitter and Facebook are really helping to build the Navarro brand.

Results: The Client is thrilled with the site in terms of design and user experience as well as brand building and global sales. Results the first month: over 12,000 pageviews; over 3,500 views on the Navarro YouTube Channel; 11-page thread on the online forum SaxOnTheWeb; over 118 mouthpieces sold worldwide. Results the first year: over 27,000 visitors and 160,000 pageviews; over 35,000 YouTube Channel views; over 4,000 Facebook likes; 100,000 hits on "SaxOnTheWeb"; and recognized as Communication Arts' webpick of the day.

208 PYTHON TAKES OVER BILLBOARD SPACE | Ad Agency: PP+K
Executive Creative Director: Tom Kenney | Creative Director: Michael Schillig
Copywriter: Michael Schillig | Art Director: Palmer Holmes | Client: The Florida Aquarium

Credits & Commentary

Assignment: The Florida Aquarium was adding a "Pythons — Florida Invaders Exhibit," featuring two massive Burmese Pythons and wanted to do something in advance to arouse people's curiosity and get them talking. So our assignment was to create a teaser billboard that would run for a week to promote the coming of some very invasive Burmese Pythons.

Approach: Currently, thousands of pythons have invaded the Florida Everglades and are creating havoc there. The Florida Aquarium wanted us to emphasize the python's invasiveness on a billboard to draw awareness to the problem and get people talking. So we showed a python literally taking over and squeezing apart an available billboard space. We teased the public with a caption announcing that pythons would be invading on March 6th. On that date, we added a Florida Aquarium logo and revealed that the pythons would be invading the Wetlands Trail at the Aquarium.

Results: This dramatic billboard with a larger-than-life python squeezing it apart certainly raised curiosity among the public and got a lot of people talking and wondering about where these pythons would be invading. Once we revealed the teaser by adding a Florida Aquarium logo to the billboard, people clamored to see these pythons in person as evidenced by an increase in traffic at the Aquarium. The billboard worked with other advertising components to create excitement for and raise attendence of this new exhibit.

210 SAND TIGER SHARK TEETH | Ad Agency: PP+K
Executive Creative Director: Tom Kenney | Creative Director: Michael Schillig
Copywriter: Michael Schillig | Art Director: Trushar Patel | Photographer: Palmer Holmes
Client: The Florida Aquarium

Assignment: The Florida Aquarium offers visitors the opportunity to get within inches of endless incredible sea creatures. Our assignment was to create some posters that would promote the arrival of the new Sand Tiger Sharks and play up this "closeness" feature in a truly unique way that would get consumers' attention and intrigue them to visit the Aquarium. Ideally this piece would also reinforce The Florida Aquarium's tagline, which is "Inches From Amazing."

Approach: Our approach was to create a series of nontraditional poster/stickers that would really stand out and promote the arrival of the new Sand Tiger Sharks and also convey how unbelievably close you could get to them. We designed a graphic representation of a fearsome Sand Tiger Shark's head with its mouth wide open. We die cut the mouth and then made sure we stuck the posters in interesting places around town that would really accentuate the teeth.

Results: The campaign was well liked by the Aquarium for its pure creativity and originality. It served two functions very well by promoting the arrival of the menacing looking Sand Tiger Sharks and, at the same time, emphasizing a very important feature of the Aquarium. That is, how unbelievably close you could get to these sharks, as well as over 20,000 other sea creatures. The unusual poster/stickers got a lot of attention, reinforced the Aquarium's tagline and, along with other advertising components, helped contribute to an increase in attendance at The Florida Aquarium.

216 MINI "NOT NORMAL" | Ad Agency: Butler, Shine, Stern & Partners
Creative Directors: Steve Mapp, Lyle Yetman | Associate Creative Director: Josh Leutz
Client: MINI Global
Link: http://bssp.com/category/clients/#/=&ca=353&cb=&ch=0&cl=3714&w=4422

Assignment: MINI has always been bold, cheeky and rallied people around a very disruptive small car. Its position in the marketplace was clear. In the last 10 years, MINI has released six additional models and has had to work very hard with a very small budget to establish their individual brands with a variety of model-specific stories. Although all these MINI models have been selling well, people were losing a clear picture of what the larger MINI brand stood for. What was it that united all of these cars and the people who bought them? We were tasked with developing this clear positioning to rally potential MINI owners to see beyond the individual models and remind them what they were really doing — not settling for boring alternatives. We needed to re-energize the brand in light of a heavy dose of recent competition that was attacking our brand and what we stood for.

Approach: MINI is not always a rational purchase decision for consumers. We chose to embrace this idea and tie it back to how the MINI brand always approaches the world, Not Normal. It was a philosophy the brand has always embraced, it spoke to the core of our owner population and it inspired a whole group of people who did not want to be caught dead looking average. Not Normal became our creative platform and drove everything the brand did. With media budgets that are always dwarfed by the category, we knew we had to counter that with a heavy emotional punch that weaved together a core human truth, the need to be different, and a story about the brand. We made this come to life in an anthemic spot that also extended into cinema, print pubs, online banners and dealerships.

Results: In a single :60 film, the brand's soul came to life and over six million people chose to watch it on YouTube. People talked about it on Facebook and Twitter and all the sudden, people started to remember what

MINI was all about. The Not Normal philosophy was fully embraced by the clients along with all the usual email sign offs, t-shirts and office banners. Dealers loved the idea and carried it through as the theme for an annual sales event as well. Most importantly, during the month of December, when the campaign launched, year-over-year sales in the US (it's biggest market) increased by 13 percent and MINI had its biggest sales month ever. It is easy to want to be safe, familiar and comfortable, but inspiring people to see the opportunity of being different with their next car purchase is not very normal.

218 PRICELINE 2012 BRAND CAMPAIGN "DOJO"
Ad Agency: Butler, Shine, Stern & Partners | Creative Director: Steve Mapp
Associate Creative Director: Josh Leutz | Copywriter: Lucas Zehner
Art Director: Gabrielle Tigan | Client: Priceline
Link: http://www.youtube.com/watch?v=1_2JAUB79W8

Assignment: After the Negotiator survived a bus crash and took a hiatus from the business to surf, Priceline was ready to show he was back to start a new chapter. In order to significantly drive traffic and bookings, Priceline needed to change the perception of the brand from just being a bid-only site to one that offers numerous products that are even faster and easier to use. We were tasked to create a breakthrough creative that would extend the plot of the Negotiator's story in a way that signified there was something new and different at Priceline while making the brand more modern and relevant to consumers.

Approach: We knew that the concept we came up with needed to live as a sustaining campaign that represented the next generation of Priceline. To achieve this, we introduced the Negotiator's daughter, played by actress Kaley Cuoco. Her character was created to embody the deal-making skills in her blood while focusing her craft on the new technologies and products Priceline has to offer. Instead of the strong-arm tactics her father has shown to promote Name Your Own Price, she is a pro with technology and products like Express Deals — which is a faster and easier way to get the best deal without bidding. Like many father's, the Negotiator does not fully understand or accept his daughter's new way of doing things, but is slowly coming around.

Results: This relationship has been a successful way of creatively showing old vs. new at Priceline and they are happy with the results.
- Positive Y/Y business growth for the 15 weeks on air.
- Cumulative Brand Linkage of competing ads that aired within the period.
- Brand attribution for each Priceline ad finished above the 2012 benchmark.
- Stronger Intent to Book than the 2012 Priceline and Competitive Norm.
- Press from multiple new sources including Ad Week, USA Today, Huffington Post and MSN Money.

219 GOOGLE "SMART DAD" | Ad Agency: Butler, Shine, Stern & Partners
Creative Director: Lyle Yetman | Associate Creative Director: Brian Lambert | Client: Google
Link: http://www.youtube.com/watch?v=2HQkugdXyHY

Assignment: Google was looking to expand the way people searched with Google products. The G mobile app embodies a lot of the features that simply add more dimension to the way people search. For example, the mobile search product uses voice input with voice response to the majority of the answers. In addition, the mobile search uses Google Now, which is more of a predicative tool to give you information before you ask for it.

Approach: Our strategic approach was to move Google beyond search. We had a strategy line that summarized this for the creative teams: "Google just doesn't enhance your search — Google enhances your daily life." The strategy was designed to find the higher order of search, but root it in everyday situations.

Results: None to note as of yet, but the commercials ranked extremely high in terms of Google's own testing measures.

220 OOMPH VIDEO SERIES | Ad Agency: Butler, Shine, Stern & Partners
Creative Director: Tom Coates | Art Director: Gabrielle Tigan | Copywriters: Michael Flannery, Kacey Coburn | Client: ZICO Pure Premium Coconut Water | Link: http://www.youtube.com/watch?v=PjwcTo-Tu-4&list=SPmF4RmppkXjQqb--o4Q8Bs39813Sllu-B&index=21

Assignment: Coconut water is a rapidly growing segment, competing against sodas, juices, sport drinks, energy drinks, teas and waters (both enhanced and the good old fashioned kind). While it's familiar to those living in tropical countries, it's a relatively unknown option to the majority of Americans. Starting in 2004, ZICO built its brand at a grass-roots level among a core consumer segment of yoga and triathlete enthusiasts in key markets. Beginning in 2013, ZICO is being distributed by its majority investor, The Coca-Cola Company. To support this new national distribution, it was time for ZICO to take itself beyond its base of athlete consumers and introduce the unknown brand and unfamiliar product to the masses.

Approach: We knew it was important to maintain the equity built among ZICO's original athlete fans, but also broaden its appeal to this new national presence. We knew it was important to go beyond just the functional benefits of coconut water (natural hydration and replenishment through electrolytes), giving them more meaning and an emotional benefit to the brand. Enter ZICO's new brand campaign: "Oomph." Our way of articulating not only the functional benefit of hydrating with ZICO, but also expanding it to encompass the positive energy we all have inside of us. With this new brand idea, ZICO can appeal to both the athletes looking for oomph to get through marathons and those of us just looking for some help getting through a long Monday afternoon at work. It's both inspiring and playful, in line with the target's own sense of motivation balanced with realism. It also helps ZICO stand apart from its coconut water competitors who rely on the same tropical or athletic imagery that's become expected from the category. We brought the story to life through a pool of short form online "Moments of Oomph" videos, outdoor advertising, digital partnerships with health and fitness sites, social media, a refreshed ZICO.com, retail programs and field marketing events.

Results: It's still early, but the new brand idea has given ZICO a fresh way to introduce itself to a broader audience of consumers. The online videos collectively have over 1.5 million views and most importantly sales are growing at a rapid pace.

221 OPTIMISTS TV CAMPAIGN (VIDEO) | Ad Agency: 160over90
Chief Creative Officer: Darryl Cilli | Executive Creative Director: Jim Walls, Tammo Walter
Creative Directors: Jim Poore, Kyle Arrango | Copywriter: Kyle Arrango
Producer: Cheri Appledy, Sybil McCarthy | Post Production: Lost Planet | Client: UCLA
Link: http://www.youtube.com/watch?feature=player_embedded&v=g1iG-UU6BjI

Assignment: The University of California, Los Angeles ("UCLA"), is one of the greatest and most influential universities in the nation and the world. Globally recognized, highly sought after and ranked as the most applied to school in the country, there are few universities in the world that have the gravitas of UCLA. It is home to nearly 40,000 students and 4,000 faculty who breed an infectious sense of community and a hunger to learn. UCLA impacts literally millions of people through its educational programs, health systems, arts and cultural programs, community service initiatives, research endeavors, athletics programs and more. No other institution combines academic excellence, intellectual curiosity, a sense of humility and an enhanced understanding of the world quite like UCLA. That said, 160over90 was tasked to create a campaign that would raise awareness, elevate perceptions and reposition UCLA as a world-leading institution. Despite its proven excellence and accomplishments, significant misunderstandings persisted about the level of impact UCLA has throughout the world. Decentralization of communication channels resulted in inconsistent and/or generic marketing messages. In addition, state funding continued to be cut significantly. Although UCLA only received seven percent of its total funding from the state, the perception from California taxpayers was that this amount was significantly higher and, therefore, UCLA struggled to gain public financial support. Overall, UCLA recognized the need to redefine themself in the eyes of the public. We embarked upon an image advertising campaign focused solely on changing the perception of UCLA in the minds of the community and positioning them as game changers in their field. This was done so through an integrated marketing approach, with the hero creative being the Optimist 1.0 and Optimist 2.0 videos, which were shared via broadcast, rich media banner ads and social media channels.

Approach: Through an in-depth discovery process we unearthed the core of what would become the new brand. From the moment we stepped on UCLA's campus we felt a palpable sense of optimism. Just about every student, faculty and staff member we met projected an air of informed enthusiasm. They not only knew they could make a difference, they were absolutely certain that they would. This unique and inspiring ethos became the through line of the brand we built. As we reviewed the lists of UCLA alum, we recognized the great opportunity we had to tell a cohesive, overarching optimism story through the stories of those who have come before us, those who stood up for something in the midst of naysayers, and therefore changed industries and shaped the world in which we all live today — a UCLA optimistic spirit that empowers.

Results: The ad yielded 31 million impressions via broadcast/digital, 1.8 million YouTube views, 2.1 percent first-month digital engagement rate (on 1.59 percent benchmark)

221 SWEETS PRESTITIAL | Ad Agency: MHC Studio | Chief Creative Officer: William Taylor
Art Director: William Taylor, Jason Scuderi | Music/Sound: Jae Bordley
Digital Arts/Multimedia: Jeong Suh | Client: Sweets | Link: http://vimeo.com/41920035

Assignment: In 1906, Sweets Catalog File was introduced to the architectural community and subsequently became the premier resource for architects to find building products. When Sweets moved its information online, it faced the challenge of managing the transition of revenue from a yearly print business to a competitive digital media offering where product information could be updated more frequently. Key to that transition was user marketing that drove qualified construction professionals (architects, engineers, contractors, etc.) to engage with a brand with which they were

familiar, but now in a different medium. Our assignment was to reposition Sweets as the digital destination of choice to find building products and download valuable supporting material that is required to incorporate products into architectural plans. Architects and specifiers are information gatherers and are drawn to detailed information about products and how they are put in place in buildings they admire. The advertising campaign played to their personalities by featuring celebrated buildings with detailed information on building products found in Sweets.com. We prominently placed the iconic Sweets logo and used green dots, in the same proportion and color as the logo, to call out the building products. Architects and specifiers were drawn to the information they crave and building product manufacturers were motivated to be a part of this engaging conversation by listing their products in Sweets.

Results: Shortly after the campaign ran in Architectural Record and archrecord.com, the sales team received unsolicited calls from building product manufacturers to be part of Sweets.com. Sweets experienced a 44 percent increase in new contracts from building manufacturers. Overall, content contributed by new and existing building product manufacturers increased by 48 percent. During the same period, Sweets.com registered users grew by 43 percent and content downloads increased by 44 percent. Page views per visit also increased by 56 percent.

222 ISIS LAUNCH :60 "SUPERMARKET MELTDOWN"
Ad Agency: Butler, Shine, Stern & Partners | Associate Creative Directors: Shahin Edalati,
Eric Liebhauser | Client: Isis | Link: http://www.youtube.com/watch?v=m3j-Q7hz1S0

Assignment: With the objective being to bring awareness to a new brand and technology, Isis wanted to create a television spot that would get consumers excited about the idea of everything in your wallet being now available on your phone in a fun and memorable way.

Approach: To create this spot, we chose to focus on one of the most common use cases and every day spend scenarios there is: the grocery store. To really highlight the juxtaposition of the old vs. new way to pay, we captured an epic cinematic slow motion catastrophe of what happens when mom has to fumble through her purse searching for her wallet, as opposed to simply using her Isis Mobile Wallet.

Results: To inform our approach and put a gauge on how we might perform in the marketplace for the launch of the Isis Mobile Wallet, we conducted a robust head-to-head quantitative copy test featuring our finished TV spots, our competitors' advertisements and an assortment of TV spots from other contemporary advertisers. Supermarket Meltdown outscored our competitive set and exceeded established research norms on statistically significant levels in the key measures of brand consideration, likeability and product recall. So not only was Supermarket Meltdown memorable and demonstrated brand building potential, consumers liked it.

222 FRUITSNACKIA | Ad Agency: Saatchi & Saatchi, NY | Creative Directors: Justin Ebert,
Alex Lea | Associate Creative Director: Russell Berland, Michael Sullivan
Client: FRUIT SNACKS | Links: http://youtu.be/i-TOGPaYJHo, http://youtu.be/vm2D83ZZ9zY,
http://youtu.be/xs-437jyi_I

Assignment: Create a single, all-encompassing campaign that could deliver on the fun and benefits of the three distinct Fruitsnacks products: Fruit by the Foot, Fruit Rollups and Gushers.

Approach: So here's the deal. We knew we wouldn't have enough time to go into specific detail about each individual product. So we decided to create a world that appeared to be made entirely out of all the Fruitsnacks material. (Which meant the product was always front and center in every frame of the spot.) And populate it with characters clearly made out of the three separate offerings: we had Larry the Gusher, Lloyd the Fruit Rollup and Linus the Fruit by the Foot. We'd then have these three fellas run around engaging in all sorts of crazy adventures that always highlighted the fun and deliciousness of Fruitsnacks. Weird? Yes. But a whole lot of fun. And to give this concept a truly unique look and feel, we hired Buck in NYC to handle the animation. They helped us develop the characters, made sure that everything truly felt like it had the same texture and color of Fruitsnacks and created TV spots that looked so good you'd want to lick the screen. It's been a great collaboration. And it's led to work that truly stands out when you see it on television.

Results: Base Turns are one of the most important metrics in CPG when it comes to connecting consumer communications with in-market efficacy. Base Turns are a measure of total volume sold per store. This metric gives a read on advertisings' effect on the business and eliminates for other business issues which may be affecting sales, but for which advertising cannot control (like distribution). This campaign has increased base turns by 9.5 percent, with positive base turns being seen across all three brands for each week the campaign was live. This campaign also garnered over 1.6 million views online and consumers spent more than twice as long on Fruitsnackia. com than comparable sites.

Index

Index

Winners Directory

PLATINUM WINNERS

3e The Life Time Agency
thelifetimeagency.com
2902 Corporate Place
Chanhassen, MN 55317 US
Tel 952 229 7114
tlatvala@lifetimefitness.com

BRIGHT RED\TBWA
www.brightredbwa.com
1821 Miccosukee Commons Drive
Tallahassee, FL 32308 US
Tel 850 668 6824
jsaler@brightredtbwa.com

Butler, Shine, Stern & Partners
www.bssp.com
20 Liberty Ship Way
Sausalito, CA 94965 US
Tel 415 331 6049
info@bssp.com

LLOYD&CO
www.lloydandco.com
180 Varick Street, Suite 1018
New York, NY 10014 US
Tel 212 414 3100
info@lloydandco.com

PP+K
www.uniteppk.com
1102 North Florida Avenue
Tampa, FL 33602 US
Tel 813 496 7000
mschillig@uniteppk.com

Publicis Kaplan Thaler
www.publiciskaplan.com
1675 Broadway
New York, NY 10019 US
Tel 917 344 7585
ryan.mcnally@pkt.com

Saatchi & Saatchi, LA
www.saatchi.com
3501 Sepulveda Boulevard
Torrance, CA 90505 US
Tel 310 214 6000
firstname.lastname@saatchila.com

GOLD WINNERS

Butler, Shine, Stern & Partners
www.bssp.com
20 Liberty Ship Way
Sausalito, CA 94965 US
Tel 415 331 6049
info@bssp.com

Charit Art
www.charitpusiri.com
415/1 Soi Ladprao 107 Bangkapi
Bangkok, Thailand 10240
Tel 66 81 642 3922
airit.art@gmail.com

DRIVEN
www.drivensolutionsinc.com
320 West Nine Mile Road, Suite B
Ferndale, MI 48220 US
Tel 248 548 3393
jcymbal@drivensolutionsinc.com

FOX Broadcasting Company
www.fox.com
10201 West Pico Boulevard
Los Angeles, CA 90064 US
Tel 310 369 1000
jessica.wassom@fox.com

Goodby Silverstein & Partners
www.goodbysilverstein.com
720 California Street
San Francisco, CA 94108 US
Tel 415 392 0669
awards@gspsf.com

Leo Burnett
www.leoburnett.com
300 Park Avenue South, 7th Floor
New York, NY 10010 US
Tel 646 840 8350
joumana.abu-shaheen@leoburnett.com

Lewis Communications
www.lewiscommunications.com
600 Corporate Parkway, Suite 200
Birmingham, AL 35242 US
Tel 205 980 0774
bfine@lewiscommunications.com

Meers
www.meers.com
1811 Walnut
Kansas City, MO 64108 US
Tel 816 474 2920
info@meers.com

omdr Co.,Ltd.
www.omdr.co.jp
202, 6-12-10, minamiaoyama
minato-ku Tokyo 1070062 JP
Tel 81 3 5766 3410
desk@omdr.co.jp

Peter Mayer Advertising
www.peteramayer.com
318 Camp Street
New Orleans, LA 70130 US
Tel 504 581 7191
mayerj@peteramayer.com

Schneider/Waibel
www.schneider-waibel.de
Neckarstraße 237
70190 Stuttgart, DE
Tel 49 711 993380
us@schneider-waibel.de

Serve
www.servemarketing.org
223 North Water Street, Suite 400
Milwaukee, WI 53202 US
Tel 414 289 0881
garym@bvk.com

STIR, LLC
www.stirstuff.com
135 West Wells Street, Suite 800
Milwaukee, WI 53203 US
Tel 414 278 0040
brianb@stirstuff.com

The Gate
www.thegateworldwide.com/ny
11 East 26th Street
New York, NY 10010 US
Tel 212 508 3400
david.bernstein@
thegateworldwide.com

The Richards Group
www.richards.com
8750 North Central Expressway
Dallas, TX 75231-6437 US
Tel 214 891 5700
jodi_phillip@richards.com

Wong, Doody, Crandall, Wiener
www.wdcw.com
1011 Western Ave, Suite 900
Seattle, WA 98104 US
Tel 206 624 5325
lara.johannsen@wdcw.com

Zulu Alpha Kilo
www.zulualphakilo.com
260 King Street E B101
Toronto, ON M5A 4L5 CA
Tel 416 777 9858
ineedanewagency@
zulualphakilo.com

SILVER WINNERS

160over90
www.160over90.com
One South Broad Street, 10th Floor
Philadelphia, PA 19107 US
Tel 215 732 3200

BRIGHT RED\TBWA
www.brightredbwa.com
1821 Miccosukee Commons Drive
Tallahassee, FL 32308 US
Tel 850 668 6824
jsaler@brightredtbwa.com

Butler, Shine, Stern & Partners
www.bssp.com
20 Liberty Ship Way
Sausalito, CA 94965 US
Tel 415 331 6049
info@bssp.com

Goodby Silverstein & Partners
www.goodbysilverstein.com
720 California Street
San Francisco, CA 94108
Tel 415 392 0669
awards@gspsf.com

Howard, Merrell & Partners
www.merrellgroup.com
8521 Six Forks Road, 4th Floor
Raleigh, NC 27615 US
Tel 919 848 2400
sstyons@merrellgroup.com

Ice House Design Ltd.
www.icehousedesign.co.uk
Canton Studios, Cleveland Reach
Bath BA1 5DB UK
Tel 01225 466 080
jack@icehousedesign.co.uk

Lewis Communications
www.lewiscommunications.com
600 Corporate Parkway, Suite 200
Birmingham, AL 35242 US
Tel 205 980 0774
bfine@lewiscommunications.com

LLOYD&CO
www.lloydandco.com
180 Varick Street, Suite 1018
New York, NY 10014 US
Tel 212 414 3100
info@lloydandco.com

Lowe Vietnam
www.lowevietnam.com
13th Harbour View Tower
35 Nguyen Hue Blvd, District 1
Hochiminh City, VN
Tel 84 8 3914 1765
info@lowevietnam.com

Meers
www.meers.com
1811 Walnut
Kansas City, MO 64108 US
Tel 816 474 2920
info@meers.com

Mekanism
www.mekanism.com
520 Broadway, 5th Floor
New York, NY 10012 US
Tel 212 226 2772
kate.dubose@mekanism.com

MHC Studio
www.construction.com
61 Pierrepont Street, 43
Brooklyn, NY 11201 US
Tel 917 439 6516
william.taylor@mhfi.com

Michael Schwab Studio
www.michaelschwab.com
108 Tamalpais Avenue
San Anselmo, CA 94960 US
Tel 415 257 5792
studio@michaelschwab.com

Pentagram Design
www.pentagram.com
204 Fifth Avenue
New York, NY 10010 US
Tel 212 683 7000
info@pentagram.com

PP+K
www.uniteppk.com
1102 North Florida Avenue
Tampa, FL 33602 US
Tel 813 496 7000
mschillig@uniteppk.com

Publicis Kaplan Thaler
www.publiciskaplan.com
1675 Broadway
New York, NY 10019 US
Tel 917 344 7585
ryan.mcnally@pkt.com

Saatchi & Saatchi, NY
www.saatchiny.com
375 Hudson Street
New York, NY 10014 US
Tel 212 463 2000
firstname.lastname@
saatchiny.com

The CementBloc
www.thecementbloc.com
641 Avenue of the Americas
New York, NY 10011 US
Tel 212 524 6200
info@thebloc.com

Zulu Alpha Kilo
www.zulualphakilo.com
260 King Street E B101
Toronto, ON M5A 4L5 CA
Tel 416 777 9858
ineedanewagency@
zulualphakilo.com

MERIT WINNERS

160over90
Bailey Lauerman
BBDO Proximity Minneapolis
Beacon/Leo Burentt Tokyo
Bold Worldwide
BRIGHT RED\TBWA
Butler, Shine, Stern & Partners
BVK
DeVito/Verdi

Elixir
Extra Credit Projects
Goodby Silverstein & Partners
Greenfield/Belser LTD
Heat SF
Hub Strategy
Hy Connect
Leo Burnett
Lewis Communications

MacLaren McCann
Mangos
McCann Detroit
MHC Studio
New Moment New Ideas Company Y&R
Pentagram
Peter Mayer Advertising
Populicom, Inc.
PP+K

Proof
Proof Advertising
Publicis Kaplan Thaler
QG Propaganda
RBMM
RBMM/The Richards Group
S.O. Creative
Saatchi & Saatchi, New York
Serve

Shine United
The CementBloc
The Gate
The Richards Group
Zulu Alpha Kilo

Design Annual 2014

GraphisDesignAnnual2014

PLATINUM WINNERS:

Lorenc+Yoo Design
Vanderbyl Design
Dankook University
IF Studio
SDG/Inne Design
Pentagram
Stranger&Stranger
Sandstrom Partners

2014   *Trim: 8.5 x 11.75"*
Hardcover: 256 pages   *ISBN: 978-1-932026-85-6*
200-plus color illustrations   *US $120*

Graphis Design Annual 2014 is the eminent international showcase of premiere work produced in all areas of contemporary graphic and digital design. Featuring full-page layouts of the best in creative excellence and innovation, this book covers categories including annual reports, branding, posters, events and more. In these pages you will find Q&As with select companies, as well as complete credits and commentary that delves deep into each work. The result is an indispensable resource for all design professionals and their clients.

Poster Annual 2014

GraphisPosterAnnual2014

PLATINUM WINNERS:

Marcos Minini
Alex Normanton
Stephan Bundi
Cold Open
Kuokwai Cheong
Raymond Tam
João Machado
Fons Hickmann
&Bjoern Wolf
Tetsuro Minorikawa
Otmar Grissemann

2014   *Trim: 8.5 x 11.75"*
Hardcover: 256 pages   *ISBN: 978-1-932026-83-2*
200-plus color illustrations   *US $120*

Poster Annual 2014 features award-winning submissions of the most compelling posters of the year, selected from the 100 Best in the Americas, the 100 Best in Asia and the 100 Best in Europe and Africa. The 2014 Annual includes an interview with **Marcos Minini**, the Associate Creative Director of Brainbox Strategic Design. Minini's inspirational work, along with the best entries in each country, state and province, help provide context for the scope of progress in the style, form and technique of international design.

Branding 6

GraphisBranding6

8 EXCEPTIONAL BRANDING CASE STUDIES:

Pentagram
WAX
People Design
Cue
Firewood Inc.
The General Design
Studio International
Alt Group

2013   *Trim: 8.5 x 11.75"*
Hardcover: 256 pages   *ISBN: 1-932026-78-8*
200-plus color illustrations   *US $120*

This book presents interviews, company profiles and visual histories of some of the biggest names in design and retail today, including: Q&A with **Pentagram, WAX, People design, Cue, Firewood, The General Design Co., Studio International** and **Alt Group**. All that, plus hundreds of images from the year's Graphis Gold Award-winning branding campaigns. This is a must-have for anyone interested in successful, creative branding — designers, businesses, students and fans alike.

Photography Annual 2013

2013   *Trim: 8.5 x 11.75"*
Hardcover: 256 pages   *ISBN: 1-932026-78-8*
200-plus color illustrations   *US $120*

Photography2013 is a moving collection of the years best photographs. Shot by some of the world's most respected photographers and selected from an international pool of entries, these beautifully reproduced images are organized by category for easy referencing. This year's book includes an interview with photographer **Bill Diadato**, discussing his background and the inspiration behind his work.

New Talent Annual 2013

GraphisNewTalentAnnual2013

Our grads not only have to be creative and smart, they must work well with others, speak well and write well... and they need to be communicators.

Kristin Sommese, *Professor*

2013   *Trim: 7 x 11.75"*
Hardcover: 256 pages   *ISBN: 1-932026-76-4*
200-plus color illustrations   *US $120*

The Graphis New Talent series is an original collection of the year's best student work. This edition features an interview with **Kristin Breslin Sommese** and **Lanny Sommese**, who belong to the graphic design faculty at Pennsylvania State University. They are an inspiration to emerging professionals in the field of Design and Advertising. The New Talent Annual serves to recognize the creative work of the best and brightest and we hope this collection will be an inspirational resource. All featured entries receive a Graphis Gold Award and a select few are chosen for the Graphis Platinum Award.

Advertising Annual 2013

Graphis Best in Advertising 2013

Many a small thing has been made large by the right kind of advertising. Mark Twain, *Roughing It (1872, 1899)*

2013   *Trim: 8.5 x 11.75"*
Hardcover: 256 pages   *ISBN: 1-932026-79-5*
200-plus color illustrations   *US $120*

Graphis Advertising 2013 presents some of the top campaigns of the year selected from hundreds of entries. Featured are seasoned works from accomplished advertising agencies, such as **Goodby, Silverstein & Partners, Bailey Lauerman, BVK, DeVito/Verdi, HOOK** and **Saatchi & Saatchi**. Each spread presents the work with a case study description written by each agency. These campaigns provide insight into the agency's creative process and how they met the needs of their clients.

www.Graphis.com

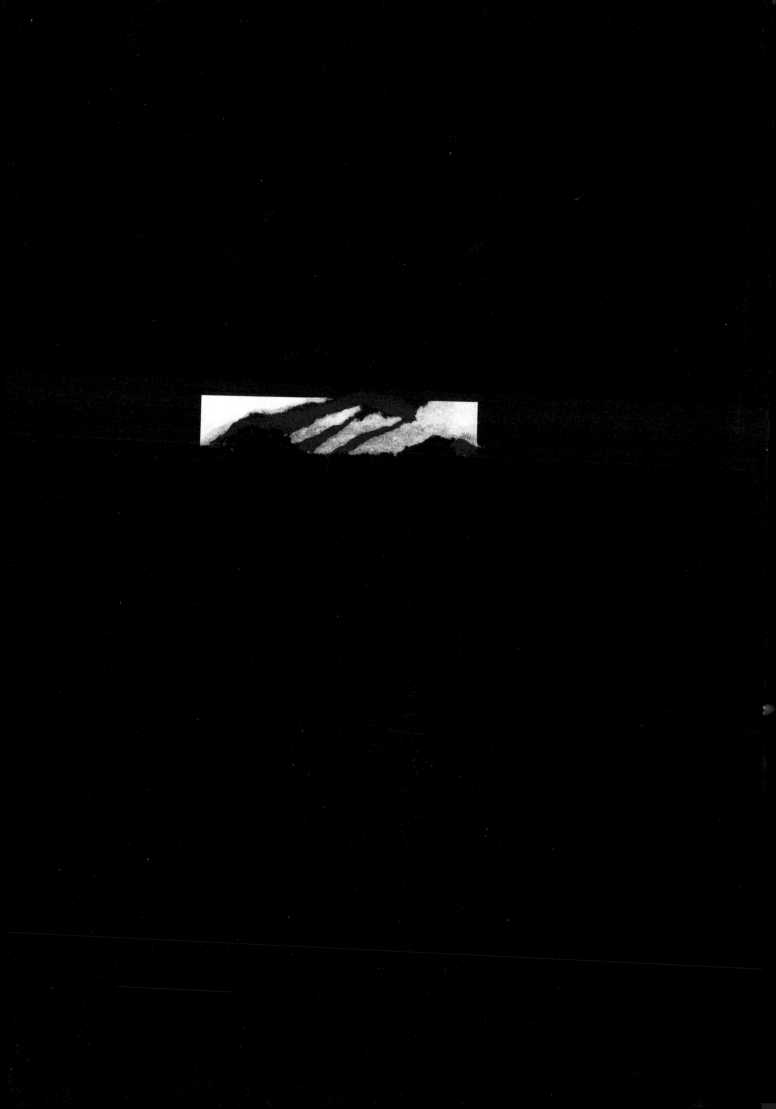